The Business Case for Love

Marc Cox

The Business Case for Love

How Companies Get Bragged About Today

Marc Cox
The Company Spirit
Gerrards Cross, UK

ISBN 978-3-030-36425-0   ISBN 978-3-030-36426-7   (eBook)
https://doi.org/10.1007/978-3-030-36426-7

This Palgrave Macmillan imprint is published by the registered company Springer Nature Switzerland AG.
The registered company address is: Gewerbestrasse 11, 6330 Cham, Switzerland

To Karen, Oliver and Sophie.
Without whom all the right words would have been in the book, but not
necessarily in the right order.

Acknowledgements

Given that my whole philosophy is based on love, the really good news is that I have loved writing this book. It is a reflection of what I do and what I believe in. Whilst writing is essentially a solitary experience, this has been a team effort. A special thanks to my wife Karen, son Oliver and daughter Sophie. All of whom have helped to give some structure to the book, edit it and correct my at times random punctuation.

Thanks go to Martin Mackay, who was the first person to read what I was writing. He was based in Singapore at the time, so I would wake up to his words of encouragement. To Paul Barnet, who suggested I write the book and was somewhat surprised when I went off and did it! To my Editorial Director, Stephen Partridge, who became a convert and backed the idea. Finally, to Camille and Marion, whose gîte in Moncravel, France, Karen and I stayed in when the pressure was on to meet the agreed deadline. It rained all weekend, I could not work the TV, and the internet stopped. Perfect conditions to knuckle down and get the book over the line!

Contents

List of Figures

1

Introduction

The alarm goes off. It is 6.10 am on 23 September 2019. My wife Karen and I have a quick cup of tea in advance of our 7am cycle spinning class and I switch on the news. The lead story is the not unexpected overnight collapse of the travel company Thomas Cook. Moments later a recording of Peter Frankhauser, the Swiss-born CEO of Thomas Cook Group, is aired, in which he announces the liquidation of the company.[1] He apologises to his 21,000 employees. He then says sorry to all his customers and finally to the hotels and all the other suppliers. He does not say sorry for taking £8.3 million in salary and benefits since he took the helm in 2014.

The following day, *The Times*, *The Daily Mail*, *The Daily Express* and *The Daily Mirror* all have this as their lead story, expressing their anger at the 'fat cats'. For the millions of pounds that he and the rest of the Board have received, with estimates of pay and perks ranging from £20 million as stated in *The Times*[2] to £47 million as stated in *The Daily Mail*.[3] Even Brexit was knocked off the front page of the morning newspapers.

In the immediate aftermath, reporters pointed towards too much debt, about £2 billion when the pension deficit was included, the weakness of sterling and even the heat wave of 2018. Perhaps these were the contributing factors, but my mind went back to the early summer of 2015, when the same Peter Fankhauser refused to apologise at the inquest for Thomas Cook Group's role in the death of two children. Christi and Bobby Shepherd had died of carbon monoxide poisoning whilst on holiday in Greece in 2006.[4] At the same hearing a previous CEO of Thomas Cook, Manny Fontenla-Novoa, simply refused to answer the questions being asked by the coroner. Only later,

© The Author(s) 2020
M. Cox, *The Business Case for Love*, https://doi.org/10.1007/978-3-030-36426-7_1

after the inquest had found that the two children were unlawfully killed, did Peter Frankhuaser apologise on behalf of Thomas Cook.

I believe that there is a direct link between the refusal to apologise and the liquidation of the company four and a bit years later, as it shines a light on not just the self-serving behaviour of the bosses involved, but the culture prevalent within the company. Not apologising, presumably on the advice of their lawyers, until forced to by the coroner, showed a complete lack of care and sensitivity towards the parents of the two children involved, who were Thomas Cook customers. Given that the premise behind their well-known advertising line 'Don't Just Book It. Thomas Cook It' was customer care, the complete lack of it caused significant damage to the reputation of the company. It left me wondering if that is how they treated the parents of two dead children, what was their mindset towards their customers and their employees? During the weeks that followed the liquidation it became quite clear that there was a lot of love amongst the employees for each other and the company, but not for the bosses at the top.

Thomas Cook is by no means alone as a company with the wrong set of values, and what could be imagined as a fairly rotten culture to be part of. As the events over the last 10 years but particularly since the financial Armageddon of 2008 have shown, never has the link between a combination of poor leadership, company behaviours, brand reputation, the customer experience and 'money in the till' (long-term sustainable growth) been more clear. Companies and their leaders frequently make the front pages of the mainstream media for the wrong reasons. These companies and their bosses are shown to be stuck in an outmoded way of working. This rogues gallery includes BP, VW, British Airways, United Airlines and Oxfam to name just six, not including the banks. Household names which people used to believe in. Over the same period many of our most cherished institutions in the UK, including the BBC and the National Health Service, have been found wanting. Perhaps most significant of all is how people now feel about our politicians, many of whom have been exposed as liars in the run-up to the Brexit referendum, and the subsequent three years. Leaving people asking the question, who can you trust?

Yet at the same time, as many companies are struggling to survive or have collapsed, others are thriving. We seem to be in a world of winners and losers, with few just bumbling along in the middle. As a consequence of this breakdown in trust, the expectations of customers and employees have changed. People want more from work than 'just a job'. Customers also want more. They want to believe in the company they are spending their money with. The companies who are winning understand this shift. Whether they operate on a global, regional or local level. They recognise the importance of creating sustainable relationships with their customers through building trust. These companies embrace a philosophy where they set out to create enjoyable, sometimes memorable, but rarely just okay customer experiences. They also know that if they want their customers to 'love' the experience on the outside, this needs to start on the inside, with their employees loving what they do, engaged around the companies values, beliefs and sense of purpose. Clear about what the Company and its Brand stands for, what makes it different and how it needs to behave.

These are the ones that get bragged about.

This is the philosophy and approach I call the Business Case for Love. Where I unashamedly make the absolute link between the love employees and customers feel for a company and its long-term commercial success. In short, the opposite of what has happened at Thomas Cook. It is the underlying way I work with my clients through my company, The Company Spirit, and it is the title of this book. One that has been some 40 years in the making. It has turned out to be more autobiographical than I first intended. Mainly because the guiding principles I use today have been honed out of the experiences I have had throughout my career and my life. The people I have met, the places I have been, the views of my family, the companies I have worked with, have all played a role in forging my beliefs.

I have tried to make the book as readable and enjoyable as possible. I am no fan of the 'business book' as so many come across as cold, turgid and a little preachy. I do enjoy reading books written by or about people I admire, Steve Jobs, at Apple, Ed Cutmull at Pixar, Phil Knight at Nike, Howard Schultz at Starbucks and the Google 'Boys': Sergey Brin and Larry Page. I have been influenced by the writing style of UK journalists Robert Peston and Tim Shipman. I hope it appeals to a wide range of people from differing ages, backgrounds and interests. I am not expecting the reader to agree with everything I have written, but the very least I hope is that it will give some fresh insights and perspectives on how they and their company behave. Whether the reader is a CEO or someone who has just entered the world of work.

There are three parts to the book, and whilst each chapter can be read in isolation, I would recommend the more standard approach of starting at the beginning and finishing at the end rather than dipping in and out.

Part I, titled 'How to Kill the Company Spirit', focusses on the mess in which much business and politics now finds itself.

Successive scandals in the UK, Europe, the USA and Japan have rocked the reputation of business and those CEOs responsible. For them, sorry seems to be the hardest word, with their lack of accountability fuelling mistrust amongst employees and customers alike.

All of which gives even more reason why employees want to believe in the company they work for and to feel proud of it. They want it to have some ethics and beliefs and they want to feel valued by their company. Yet according to research by Gallup, a staggering 87% of employees are not engaged. Is the traditional command and control form of leadership to blame? Are the current MBA schools producing the wrong type of leader? Good at the 'head' part but struggling with the 'heart' side, and thereby out of touch with the needs of employees today. By drawing on personal experience (either as a customer or as an employee) with British Airways, WH Smith, Toys 'R' Us, Mothercare and BHS, I examine how these companies stop looking after what makes them different and embark instead on a race to the bottom. An emphasis on transactional behaviour which leads to little or no customer experience, and in time, no business. They are run by people who have little idea as to how to create companies that are loved by their employees, and their customers.

These are the ones who kill the Company Spirit.

In Part II, titled 'Falling in Love', I suggest how companies need to behave to get bragged about.

By retracing the ups and downs of a career starting in advertising and then progressing onto marketing and Consulting, I illustrate how these experiences shaped what would become the unique philosophy and approach called the 'Business Case For Love'. I draw on anecdotes from work in Europe, the USA and the Far East to explain why my focus is now on company culture. And how one simple question, 'What is a customer experience you love?', starts people on a journey to behaving differently in business.

I look at why almost every company judges itself exclusively against their immediate competitors but as customers we don't. Why we judge a company against our own roller deck of personal experiences and how we as individuals are very clear as to what makes a memorable customer experience.

Hence part of the philosophy and approach with my clients is to help them take the blinkers off and inspire them to behave as a 'Best In Class' company, not just 'Best in Category'. I have come to the conclusion that there are six 'best in class' company behaviours which really do separate the best from the rest. Each one is shared and brought to life through observations and experiences.

'Love', perhaps not surprisingly, is a polarising word in business. That is why it is central to my beliefs, philosophy and approach. It is what my clients buy into. The 'Love Grid' is a unique yet quick and simple way of explaining the role love can play in business. It shows the link between the internal company behaviour, normally set by the bosses, and the consequential customer experience and customer relationship. The 'Love Grid' illustrates the three different types of behaviour found within business (the 'Dealer', the 'Retailer', the 'Brand') and how this affects how we feel about the company in question. Is the experience ok, enjoyable or memorable? Is my relationship with the company transactional, respectful or based on love? And why is the middle no longer a safe place to be?

Drawing on experiences with clients in a range of categories (Automotive, Banks and Insurance Companies, Fashion, Food, Manufacturing, Technology and Transport) across Germany, Sweden, the UK and the USA, I use the last chapter in Part II to demonstrate how to create a Company Spirit. The Company Spirit Model is what I call my signature dish, and its primary role is to create clarity around what a company stands for. My job is to help guide and facilitate its birth. Unlike many consultancies, I start from the belief that the answer is in my client, not in me. It is through the very act of a team creating their Company Spirit that their beliefs, ownership clarity and a commitment to bring it to life manifest themselves. This is the mindset that kicks off cultural change. It illustrates the importance of 'Roots' and how this is the anchor for the whole of the Company Spirit. Each Company Spirit is by definition unique, as no brand or company is the same. Each has its story to tell, and when told in a genuine, honest way, it means the company culture is grounded in authenticity. One which employees get and customers feel.

Part III is titled 'Staying in Love' and discusses how this requires the boss to behave as a 'best in class' leader. To be crystal clear, this is a sea change from those who operate with a command and control approach, or whose primary driver is 'I' not 'we'. As with company behaviours, I believe there are six leadership behaviours which separate the best from the rest, and I highlight these through discussing some heroes and villains, as well as bringing in examples from my own clients. This framework acts as a guide for the reader to gain fresh thinking about their own behaviours and what they need to change if they aspire to be loved by their own employees.

There follows a practical guide on how to engage and embed the Company Spirit to reach all parts of the business, and why the location, venue and the running order of the Company Spirit Event really do matter.

Love is a strong emotional and mental state. To create and share love, first amongst employees, and then extending out to customers, leaders must be able to embrace the same basic principles that make a marriage and a relationship work over the long term. A marriage starts with mutual attraction and lust, which later becomes a sense of attachment and bonding. A Company Spirit journey follows a similar path. The initial phase is about generating an attraction between the company and its employees, and just like in real life, this can be quick to happen. To do this, it needs to provoke an emotion. A spark and frisson of excitement about the company they work for. It's what I mean by starting with the 'heart' and then following with the 'head'. Without this, the relationship is more rational, more a friend than a lover. Still important but not quite the same.

Sharing and maintaining this love is about creating the right environment to keep this flame alive. As with marriage it is where the hard work begins to turn the initial attraction into a sense of belonging. This is where the 'head' starts to play more of a role, and the term I use to make sure this sense of belonging sticks is 'embed'. There are four levers I recommend to my clients to achieve this, and we look at each one in turn.

The aspiration is to create an authentic culture which employees and customers love, and my summary chapter takes the reader though not just the steps, but the order in which to take them. It finishes with a series of testimonials (love stories) from a variety of CEOs sharing the results of their own Company Spirit Journey, and the impact it had on them both personally and for the company they led.

Building a strong Company Spirit based on love requires a revolutionary philosophy and leadership style. The blinkers need to come off and a new wave of thinking embraced. Those who are stuck in their ways will find this a challenge. Those who are curious and seeking new ideas will feel invigorated.

This book is a transformational experience, certainly for the author and hopefully for the reader. Let the journey begin.

Notes

1. 'Thomas Cook CEO on Liquidation: "I Apologise"', Reuters, 23 September 2019, https://in.reuters.com/article/us-thomas-cook-grp-ceo/thomas-cook-ceo-on-liquidation-i-apologise-idINKBN1W8024
2. 'PM attacks pay for Thomas Cook bosses', *The Times,* 23 September 2019, https://www.thetimes.co.uk/article/thomas-cook-board-received-20m-in-five-years-j8ll0zjt8
3. 'Greed of the Thomas Cook fat cats', *The Daily Mail,* 23 September 2019, https://www.dailymail.co.uk/news/article-7495919/Thomas-Cook-fat-cats-creamed-47MILLION-pay-perks.html
4. 'Corfu carbon monoxide inquest: Thomas Cook "breached duty of care"', *The Independent,* 13 May 2015, https://www.independent.co.uk/news/uk/crime/corfu-carbon-monoxide-inquest-thomas-cook-breached-duty-of-care-over-deaths-of-bobby-and-christi-10247179.html

Part I

How to Kill the Company Spirit

2

Leadership in the Dock

If you have not seen *The Big Short* then take a look. It takes aim at the reasons behind the financial crisis of 2007–2008 and what happened afterwards. Be sure to watch it all the way through because the most telling part is the epilogue. The film suggests that bankers by the dozen were jailed and the big banks broken up. Except of course they were not. The big banks survived to fight another day, leaving the rest of us to get angry and lose trust in the system.

In the 10 years since the financial crisis, banks had been fined a staggering $321 billion.[1] The rogues gallery includes HSBC, UBS, JPMorgan, Standard Chartered, ING, RBS, Goldman Sachs, Credit Suisse, ABN Amro and Barclays, to name but a few. There is still no sign of an end to this. The UK-based regulator, the Financial Conduct Authority, imposed 10 fines worth a total of £320 million in the six months to the end of June 2019.[2] The biggest fine in 2019 was the £102 million levied on Standard Chartered for failing to combat money laundering and £45.5 million for Bank of Scotland's failure to disclose information about a £245 million fraud at its Reading Branch. To normal human beings these are simply staggering figures. The banks are constantly being fined, and just as the writers of *The Big Short* predicted, little seems to have changed.

Of course, it's not just the banks. Terrifyingly, fines are also affecting that supposedly most treasured of UK institutions, the National Health Service. Late 2017 saw Shrewsbury and Telford Hospital Trust fined following the deaths of five elderly patients.[3] In the spring of 2018, Southern Health NHS Foundation was fined £2 million[4] after a series of management failings led to the deaths of two vulnerable patients at different facilities owned by the Trust. These incidents were accompanied by little sign of tangible personal

© The Author(s) 2020
M. Cox, *The Business Case for Love*, https://doi.org/10.1007/978-3-030-36426-7_2

accountability from those at the top, but more of the usual platitudes. 'We are sorry' and 'Lessons have been learned'.

In 2017, Rolls Royce was fined £671 million[5] to settle wide-ranging allegations of corruption in Indonesia, Russia, China, Nigeria and Brazil. BP was fined $20.8 billion for the Deepwater Horizon oil spill on top of the $28 billion[6] spent on the clean-up and compensation. Finally, whilst tiny in comparison, EE were fined the relatively trifling amount of £2.7million[7] for overcharging its customers. EE said in a statement that it 'unreservedly' apologises to those customers affected.

Over in Japan and between 2012 and 2015, the optical maker Olympus,[8] the airbag maker Takarta and the then conglomerate Toshiba all suffered scandals ranging from a company-wide accounting fraud to a massive safety cover-up involving multiple fatalities. During 2017 and 2018 Nissan Motor, Suburu, Tooray Industries, Kobe Steel and Mitsubishi Materials[9,10,11] all admitted to cheating on quality tests or falsifying documents to sell products of lower quality than stated. In December 2017, the unthinkable happened to one of the nation's proudest achievements. The Hakata-to-Tokyo bound Shinkansen,[12] or Bullet Train, pulled into Nagoya and a thousand passengers were ordered off the train. There was a burning smell and unusual sounds, which a later investigation found to be from cracks in the chassis. This proved to be a tipping point in the Land of the Rising Sun, and led many to question what had gone wrong with the way their companies operated. How could these mistakes happen? Moreover, how could they occur with those at the top not knowing what was happening within their own organisations? And if people did know, what type of leadership allows this to happen?

We now know that the roots of 'Dieselgate' at VW started when the then CEO, Martin Winterkorn, committed the company to becoming the world's number one car manufacturer. To do that, the company had to 'crack' the USA. To do that, they needed to build larger cars favoured by Americans as well as complying with the Obama administration's toughening standards on safety and emissions. To do that, they decided to cheat on emissions tests by rewarding drivers with better mileage, at the same time as avoiding expensive and cumbersome pollution-control systems. So, even though it was suggested early on in the investigation by Michael Horn, President and CEO of the VW Group of America, when in front of a House Committee at Congress, that the actual actions were 'of a few rogue engineers', time has shown that a corporate culture of cheating was led from the top.[13]

When an organisation or an institution fails, it is the leadership, not the employees, who are the root cause. They set the goals and the strategy and through their behaviours define the culture of the company. 'The fish rots from the head down' is an ancient proverb that could not be more relevant today. This proverb captures precisely what happens within a company. Something rotten must have happened within the culture of United Airlines for its employees to think it was okay to drag Dr. Dao off United Express Flight 3411 on 9 April 2017[14] at O'Hare International, Chicago. The doctor was filmed by other passengers on their mobiles screaming as he was pulled from his seat, hitting his face in the process before being dragged, apparently unconscious, off the plane. What must have gone wrong in a company for employees at various Japanese companies or VW to think it is acceptable to cheat on quality tests or falsify documents to sell products of lower quality than stated? Why do hugely well-known institutions think it is alright to cover up their sins from the past? In almost every case the actions of the employees involved are a direct consequence of the behaviour of the leadership, the culture they create, and the financial and strategic goals behind them.

This brings us to Fred Goodwin, the CEO of RBS at the time of the financial crash. The poster boy for all that went wrong in the banking industry and whose actions, behaviours and leadership brought both the bank and the UK to its knees. What if he had been properly held to account, rather than just having his pension trimmed and his knighthood revoked? The threat of jail rather than a corporate fine would surely have concentrated the minds of other CEOs and perhaps changed the course of history. Would this have helped to rebuild trust amongst ordinary people who watched aghast and helpless as the crisis unfolded? This is not a totally hypothetical scenario, as there was one country which did jail its bankers: Iceland.

In February 2018, the local Icelandic newspaper, *Frettabladid*, calculated that the Icelandic judiciary had sentenced 36 bankers to a total of 96 years in prison.[15] All of the criminal cases are linked to the notorious crash of the Icelandic banking system in 2008. The man credited with achieving this is Olafur Hauksson, the police chief whose job it was to bring the bankers to task. He was interviewed both in *The Financial Times*[16] and in a special report for Sky News,[17] and when asked why Iceland did what every other country shied away from he said,

'the lesson is not to have a part of our society above the law...we have to have policing in this field of our society...you cannot say because it's a bank you have to avoid it'. Unnar Gunnarsdottir, the Director General of the Icelandic Financial Supervisory Authority, adds 'you have to remember ethics...you have to have a compass to do the right thing...you have to have a sense of what is right and wrong'. Iceland's Prime Minister, Bjarni Benediktsson, believed that the nation had lost its trust and needed to heal and reconcile. He saw jailing the bankers 'as a necessary part of rebuilding trust and getting to the bottom of what happened'.[18]

Unlike its European counterparts, Iceland meaningfully acknowledged its mistakes, reprimanded those responsible and actively chose to move forward with a clear set of moral values. The result has been a country re-energised. It is now booming again, largely down to tourism, with numbers jumping from 500,000 in 2010 to an expected 2.4 million in 2018. The International Monetary Fund has declared that Iceland has achieved economic recovery 'without compromising its welfare model'[19] or 'unduly punishing its citizens for crimes committed by its bankers'. Gross Domestic Product grew by 3.8% in the second quarter of 2019,[20] compared to the previous quarter. This new-found energy has impacted all parts of the country. Iceland was the smallest nation ever to appear at a major football finals when taking part in Euro 2016. The magazine *Reykjavik Grapevine* roared, 'And now we smite them into tiny pieces of dust and destroy their goal with a ball set on fire by our volcanic thunder'[21] and they went on to destroy England, in the round of 16, with a memorable 2–1 victory. Cheered on by their supporters, Iceland went on to play at the 2018 FIFA World Cup complete with their 'Thunder Clap' chant, which in turn was adopted by the supporters of the European team at the 2018 Ryder Cup in Paris.

Iceland not only said sorry to its people but actually did something about it. The country and its people have had a sense of closure from the events of 2008. Saying sorry is very in vogue at the moment. Banks now say sorry a lot, the Catholic Church says sorry for the behaviour of some of its priests, and the BBC kept on saying sorry when the Jimmy Savile scandal broke. The CEO of United Airlines eventually said sorry after the violent removal of the fare-paying passenger Dr. Dao. British Airways is always saying sorry: sorry for the now regular IT breakdowns, sorry for the breach of security, and sorry for the hacking of sensitive customer data. The bosses at VW said sorry for Dieselgate.

So why do I struggle to believe them? For me, it is the lack of accountability and responsibility from those at the top. This does not mean that saying sorry always needs to lead to a resignation, but rather an acknowledgement from the boss that, 'I've listened, I get it and I'll do something about it'. If there is no sense of a change in behaviour to show that lessons have really been learnt, the apology is no more than words. To say sorry is to feel regret for an action taken and to ask for forgiveness. The act in question may have been a simple mistake or a deliberate lie. We all know that it is not just saying sorry that counts, but how we say it. Perhaps that is why I am more inclined to believe the Japanese CEO rather than their western counterpart. The Japanese approach comes across as 'Sorry, we will fix it' and not 'Sorry that we got caught'.

I've been to Japan twice. There were 28 years between visits. My last trip in the early spring of 2016 took me from the powder snow of Rusutsu on the northern island of Hokkaido to the majesty of Kyoto, and the sensory overload that is Tokyo. A 10-day visit is not enough time to understand a society with deep-seated traditions that still puzzles even the most informed western eyes. Even so, I fell in love with the culture, its food and its people.

I learnt during my trip how often people bow in Japan. It is the equivalent of the handshake, the peck on the cheek or the slap on the back. Bowing is used from everything to saying hello and goodbye to showing respect and even asking a favour. Bowing in apology is the customary way for the Japanese to show contrition. The deeper and longer the bow, the sorrier you are. The Japanese have made saying sorry an art form, with at least 20 ways to do so. Not long after I returned from the trip, Mitsubishi's boss, Tetsuor Aikawa,[22] told a packed news conference he was sorry, and I believed him. Although Mr. Aikawa said he had no idea of what was going on at the company, he felt responsible and led by example. He took a very deep and long bow and seemed consumed by genuine shame at what had happened. This got me thinking. When had I seen a CEO in the West say sorry and I believed him, or occasionally, her? Almost never. The sense of those responsible 'getting away with it' is one of the reasons behind what the media and our friends the politicians rather dismissively and simplistically call 'populism': a lack of perceived fairness which fuels the sense of frustration from the knowledge that the CEOs who run companies that have transgressed, or have allowed illegal practices to happen, are not held personally responsible. When these crimes are finally investigated and perpetrators found guilty, either nothing happens or the company is fined. Some trite message is trotted out about 'lessons learnt' and 'we apologise unreservedly' and then the company continues as if nothing happened.

These CEOs rarely, if ever, appear in a criminal court to account for their decisions. Yet more and more they find themselves in the court of public opinion. This failure to act has had an unintended consequence because the constant outpouring of poor behaviour on the front pages of our newspapers undermines the trust we have in large swathes of business and their bosses. Throw in the UK Parliamentary Expenses Scandal in 2009, the lies of Brexit in 2016, the consequent poor behaviour of most UK politicians ever since, and the 'Sex for Sale' exposure at the charity Oxfam[23] and it is not surprising that because of this lack of honesty, trust in our government, politicians in general, NGOs, the media and the people who run them has not so much collapsed but been destroyed.

The failure to hold those responsible to account for their actions and behaviours did not lead to widespread civic unrest as some commentators had predicted. Instead, it led to a quiet seething amongst millions of people about this sense of lack of justice which found its voice unexpectedly some eight years on from 2008 and the time of *The Big Short*.

Notes

1. 'World's biggest banks Fined $321 billion since financial crisis', Bloomberg, 2 March 2017, https://www.bloomberg.com/news/articles/2017-03-02/world-s-biggest-banks-fined-321-billion-since-financial-crisis
2. 'City regulator fines balloon to £320 m in six months', *The Guardian*, 14 July 2019, https://www.theguardian.com/business/2019/jul/14/city-regulator-fines-balloon-to-320m-in-six-months
3. 'Shrewsbury and Telford Hospital NHS Trust fined over fall deaths', BBC News, 28 November 2017, https://www.bbc.co.uk/news/uk-england-shropshire-42155597
4. 'Southern Health fined £2 m over deaths of two patients', BBC News, 26 March 2018, https://www.bbc.co.uk/news/uk-england-43542284
5. 'Rolls-Royce to pay £671 m over bribery claims', *The Guardian*, 16 January 2017 https://www.theguardian.com/business/2017/jan/16/rolls-royce-to-pay-671m-over-bribery-claims
6. 'BP fined a record $20.8 billion for oil spill disaster', *The Verge*, 5 October 2015, https://www.theverge.com/2015/10/5/9454393/bp-oil-spill-record-fine-doj-settlement
7. 'EE fined £2.7 m for overcharging customers', *The Guardian*, 18 January 2017, https://www.theguardian.com/business/2017/jan/18/ee-fined-overcharging-ofcom-mobile-phone
8. 'Olympus Scandal', Wikipedia, https://en.wikipedia.org/wiki/Olympus_scandal
9. 'Takata Corporation', Wikipedia, https://en.wikipedia.org/wiki/Takata_Corporation
10. 'Toshiba boss quits over £780 m accounting scandal', *The Guardian*, 21 July 2015, https://www.theguardian.com/world/2015/jul/21/toshiba-boss-quits-hisao-tanaka-accounting-scandal
11. 'Japan Inc.: a corporate culture on trial after scandals', *The Financial Times*, 3 January 2018, https://www.ft.com/content/26d4843a-e743-11e7-97e2-916d4fbac0da

12. 'Japan Inc.: a corporate culture on trial after scandals', *The Financial Times*, 3 January 2018, https://www.ft.com/content/26d4843a-e743-11e7-97e2-9 16d4fbac0da

13. 'Volkswagen emissions scandal: Few rogue engineers are to blame, says VW chief executive', *The Independent*, 9 October 2015, https://www.independent.co.uk/news/business/news/volkswagen-emissions-scandal-a-few-rogue-engi-neers-are-to-blame-says-vw-chief-executive-a6687201.html

14. 'United Express Flight 3411 incident', Wikipedia, https://en.wikipedia.org/wiki/United_Express_Flight_3411_incident

15. '36 Bankers, 96 Years in Jail', *The Reykjavik Grapevine*, 7 February 2018, https://grapevine.is/news/2018/02/07/36-bankers-96-years-in-jail/

16. 'Olafur Hauksson, the man who jailed Iceland's bankers', *The Financial Times*, 9 December 2016, https://www.ft.com/content/dcdb43d4-bd52-11e6-8b45-b8b81dd5d080

17. 'Special Report: Iceland: Bankers Behind Bars', Sky News, 12 September 2017, https://www.youtube.com/watch?v=eDKmEwP-5pg

18. 'Special Report: Iceland: Bankers Behind Bars', Sky News, 12 September 2017, https://www.youtube.com/watch?v=eDKmEwP-5pg

19. 'Iceland jailed bankers and rejected austerity-and it has been a suc-cess',12 June 2015, https://www.commondreams.org/views/2015/06/12/iceland-jailed-bankers-and-rejected-austerity-and-its-been-success

20. 'GDP rises 2% in Iceland in 2nd qtr', https://countryeconomy.com/gdp/iceland

21. 'And now we smite them...' *Reykjavik Grapevine*, 14 June 2016, https://twit-ter.com/rvkgrapevine/status/742809859289190400

22. 'When saying sorry is the only thing to do', BBC News, 20 April 2016, https://www.bbc.co.uk/news/business-36093703

23. 'Timeline: Oxfam sexual exploitation scandal in Haiti', *The Guardian*, 15 June 2018, https://www.theguardian.com/world/2018/jun/15/timeline-oxfam-sexual-exploitation-scandal-in-haiti

3

The Backlash: The Establishment Gets a Bloody Nose

In the Brexit referendum of 2016 I voted to Remain, yet I was not surprised when the UK voted to Leave. I was not surprised, a few months later, when I was standing around the TV monitors at Heathrow Airport waiting for an early morning flight on 9 November 2016 watching Donald Trump astound the world by becoming President of the United States. Two seismic events on either side of the Atlantic and separated by just six months. Both were a result of a breakdown in trust and patience with the status quo.

There were large parts of the referendum campaign which made me angry. Statistics and numbers were thrown about on both sides but few seemed to understand, particularly on the Remain side, that shouting at the electorate, who after all are their customers, with dire warnings of economic catastrophe and constant referrals to experts was never going to work. Over three years on from the Referendum, never has the phrase 'There are three kinds of lies: lies, damned lies and statistics' popularised in the USA by Mark Twain felt more true.

I could see the result coming because I'm lucky in that I get to travel a lot, in the UK, Europe and beyond. I am a Londoner. Indeed I can lay claim to being a true 'Cockney' as I was born in the London Hospital on the Mile End Road of East London which was within earshot of the Bow Bells. I love London. I live not far away, but now on the west side not the east. I have worked in London all my life and have my London base at the business club One Alfred Place, just behind Tottenham Court Road in London's West End. London has changed enormously from the days when I started out in Advertising a decade or so after 'Mad Men' (the fictional series about Madison Avenue and advertising) notionally drew to a close.

© The Author(s) 2020
M. Cox, *The Business Case for Love*, https://doi.org/10.1007/978-3-030-36426-7_3

London is vibrant, energetic and creative. It is highly multicultural. It is not like the rest of the UK. Anyone who travels around the country cannot help but notice that life outside London and the South East is very different. Yes, of course, some places are thriving. Parts of Bristol, Manchester, Leeds and York come to mind. Others are not. The UK doesn't feel very comfortable in its own skin. Years of austerity imposed by the government in order to balance the books fuelled the feeling of injustice. The country feels divided: attitudinally, socially and economically. For many our best years seem to be behind us, not in front. This is the UK that most of our politicians and their media cohorts in the Westminster Bubble seemed to completely misunderstand.

Equally misunderstood in the run-up to the Referendum was the notion that people would stay tribal and support the recommendation of their traditional political party, which if they had, would have resulted in an overwhelming vote to Remain. Instead, all sorts of odd alliances occurred. Viewed through my old advertising eyes, clarity of message of the Leave Campaign 'Take Back Control' combined with people voting with their heart on emotionally loaded slogans like 'hope for a different future' won the day against a campaign of mixed and complicated messages appealing to the head. The emotionally-led strategic advert beat the rational tactical ad.

Thousands of column inches have been devoted to trying to understand the reasons behind the vote. To me the answer is simple: the consequence of not being listened to. When a company stops listening to its customers through arrogance and a belief in its own omniscience, it normally marks the beginning of a terminal decline. It's no different for politicians and political parties. I have lost count over the last 10 years of the number of times UK politicians have stated in interviews, 'we must listen more to what people are saying to us'. But they don't. They carry on as if nothing has happened. At the core of the vote lay a very human reaction. Millions of people up and down the country were silently screaming, 'You never listen to us, so why should we listen to you? The bankers, big business, our institutions, the media get away with it so why should we trust what you and your "experts say". No one ever seems to be accountable and we pay the price. We haven't got much anyway, so what have we got to lose'. The Referendum was their big chance. People wanted to give the Establishment in the UK a bloody nose and they did. The citizens of the USA repeated the message a few months later. It is somewhat ironic that Iceland, a country that sits in the Atlantic and roughly halfway between the two, had listened to their people and walked a different path. The Icelandic Leadership Team knew what to do to rebuild trust with their people to heal the wounds left by 2008 and reunite the country around a common sense of purpose, values and beliefs. Visually, the Thunder Clap physically brings two separate hands together to create one sound: a crowd in unison. It symbolises togetherness and rebuilding. There was no Thunder Clap in UK politics after the financial Armageddon, only division. Politicians along with the whole country are suffering the consequences. The UK was split on Referendum Day and remains split today.

When a company has poor leadership, the employees are usually the ones who suffer. When a country has poor leadership, its people suffer. Right now in the UK, those most guilty of an old-fashioned, outmoded way of working and behaving are our politicians, none more so than the former Prime Minister Theresa May. Beginning with the general election and then through the whole of the Brexit negotiations, the last two years have been painful to watch and experience. May's inability to mobilise the English language to convey empathy, community and sincerity for those caught up in the appalling Grenfell Tower fire was unforgivable. When a country grieves, it looks to its leaders to provide stability and hope. We look to them to harness the soul of a country to create a sense of togetherness and strength. Instead, it was Simon Cowell who rallied the music stars of the UK and turned words into action so as to provide homes and food for our neighbours. At a time when all we needed was honesty and compassion, we got empty words and false promises. More recently we have been treated to the comedy of errors that was her Brexit negotiations. She didn't vote for Brexit, so from day one led a government, Parliament and the country through a process which she did not believe in. She did not unite Parliament or her own party around what was the vision for Brexit at the outset and thus led the negotiations without a clear plan and with a disunited team. May was rooted in sound bites: 'Now is not the time' for a Scottish Referendum, 'Strong and Stable' for how she wanted to be seen as Prime Minister during the General Election, until she was dubbed the Maybot for her lack of ability to communicate on a human scale. The empty and vacuous claim of 'Brexit means Brexit' dominated the early part of the Brexit negotiations. This then morphed into the truly terrifying 'No deal is better than a bad deal'. Then the constant repeat in Parliament and on the streets of the message: 'We will leave the EU on 29th March 2019'. Which, of course the UK did not. Other than the glory of being Prime Minister, I struggled to understand how she could square what she believed in and what she did. Perhaps that's what happens to career politicians: they don't really believe in anything, they just do enough and say enough to get voted back in every five years or so.

Theresa May is not alone. We appear to have a generation of politicians over the age of 50 who seem incapable of telling the truth. When a company or politician has lied, it is an act of betrayal. The bigger the lie, the bigger the reaction amongst employees, stakeholders and customers. Trust in the relationship is broken. People feel cheated. This seems to be beyond the understanding of most politicians. They seem oblivious to the effect that constantly saying one thing and doing another has on the electorate. Why would you trust anyone who repeatedly lies? This was perfectly summed up for me on the day that the first vote on the EU Withdrawal Bill was supposed to happen in December 2018. Government Ministers trotted out in front of the cameras in the morning to say that there was no way the vote was going to be postponed. Four hours later, it had been. Is it any wonder that the trust levels in politicians are so low and they are held in such low esteem?

Now there is Boris. Perhaps the only thing that can be said for certain about Boris Johnson is that he is the very opposite of Theresa May. Being members of the Conservative Party is about the only thing they have in common. He embarked on his Prime Ministership with clarity, a sense of purpose and optimism. He too has pinned his success on an end date. 'We are getting ready to come out on October 31st. Come what may…Do or die'. Boris lives on, with his next crusade of a General Election which he duly won, with the UK finally leaving on 31 January 2020. Clarity may be over the horizon but for now no one can predict what will happen day by day let alone week by week.

Of course poor behaviour by politicians is not restricted to the UK. The Edelman Trust Barometer,[1] an annual report which charts how people are feeling across 28 different countries worldwide, confirms that this is a global problem. The chilling headline conclusion '…reveals a world of seemingly stagnant distrust. People's trust in business, government, NGOs and media remained largely unchanged from 2017: 20 of 28 markets now lie in distruster territory, up one from last year'. The report goes on to talk about how this breakdown in trust has built up over the years as a consequence of people looking at elements of the Establishment with increasing incredulity. The Edelman Trust pointed the finger at 2008–a year which changed the way a lot of people thought about big business, once-respected institutions, governments and the media.

The Edelman Trust confirms what I've thought for a long time: we lost trust in our politicians and their messages a while back. Now we don't trust even the messenger. The media is also in the dock and UK newspapers, I am ashamed to say, seem to be at the forefront of spinning a story to suit the views of their readers. I have always been aware of the political leanings of each of the UK's national newspapers, but coverage of Brexit has seen most sink to a new low with deeply unedifying headlines whose sole purpose is to push the paper's chosen perspective.

I must admit I didn't see the backlash over Facebook and Twitter and other social media sites coming. Perhaps it's a generational thing. I don't really use Facebook and I am light on Twitter. I do get a lot of my news from the Twitter feeds of our traditional media. I understood the problem of 'fake news' but underestimated the impact. Then the Cambridge Analytica data scandal broke.[2] This involved both the harvesting of personal information from 87 million Facebook users and then the use of this data to attempt to influence voter opinion on behalf of politicians who hired them. The algorithms which I thought were helpful now have their dark side exposed. I no longer feel it is okay for Amazon or Trip Advisor to email me about 'new recommendations' based on my browsing history, or for team building exercises to be advertised after I have been speaking about my latest Go-Ape adventure with my phone placed firmly face down on the table. I am not the only one to have my doubts and worries, with over six out of ten people surveyed seeing fake news as a weapon.[3]

One glimmer of hope within the report is that trust in 'proper' journalism is on the up. Journalism that is based on insights and the search for the truth rather than on opinion and hearsay. Laura Kuenssberg, the political editor of the BBC; Robert Peston, once of the BBC and now political editor of rival ITV news; and Lewis Goodall recently at Sky News, represent a new breed of journalist, with the wiriness of an old-fashioned 'newshound' whilst also being equipped for the modern-day needs of constant Twitter updates and regular, almost hourly deadlines. Robert Peston in his books *How Do We Fix This Mess?* and the more recent *WTF* describes clearly and passionately why it is now payback time for the Establishment. He was honest enough to admit that being part of the 'North London Bubble' meant that he didn't see Brexit or Trump coming down the track. He was in denial but no longer is. The fallout from 2008 shows little sign of slowing down and its consequences mean the axis of what is normal has shifted in the UK, the USA and most of Europe. No one can be sure quite how this will all play out, but one aspect is certain: much higher levels of honesty, integrity, ethics and trust are needed if the equivalent of the global Thunder Clap has a chance of bringing together what is now divided.

Business and Business Leaders have a huge role to play in this but currently, like our politicians and parts of the media, many are held in contempt. To adapt to the new normal they must start to think and behave differently. To do this they must reflect the needs of this century, not last century.

Notes

1. 2018 Edelman Trust Barometer, 21 January 2018, https://www.edelman.com/research/2018-edelman-trust-barometer
2. 'Facebook says 87 million people's data was taken in the Cambridge Analytica scandal', Business Insider, 4 April 2018, https://www.businessinsider.com/facebook-87-million-peoples-data-taken-in-cambridge-analytica-scandal-2018-4
3. 'Nearly 70 percent of people are worried about fake news as a weapon', CNBC, 22 January 2018, https://www.cnbc.com/2018/01/22/nearly-70-percent-of-people-are-worried-about-fake-news-as-a-weapon-survey-says.html

4

'But I have an MBA!'

I was on the very early flight to Stockholm early in 2018 when I read one of the best pieces of sports journalism I've read for a long time. The article, written by Matthew Syed in *The Times*,[1] headlined 'Narcissist Who Napalms Club Cultures', was about Jose Mourinho, the now ex-Manchester United manager. Yet football and football management only appeared a few paragraphs in. The writer started by talking about the collapse of Enron back in 2001 and made reference to the photograph of Kenneth Lay, the Chairman of Enron, in the company's annual report of 1997. He made the point that whilst most annual reports carried a photo of their CEO of a moderate size, the photo of Lay and also his CEO, Jeffrey Skilling, took up the entire page.

It was the next bit of the article which really stood out for me. A few years after the collapse of Enron, Arijit Chatterjee and Donald Hambrick, two management professors, took a deeper look at the link between the photo size of the leaders in company reports to see if there was a link to their leadership style and the culture of the company.

Sure enough, leaders who opted for super-sized photos were far more likely to use personal pronouns–'me', 'mine' and 'myself'–rather than collective pronouns such as 'we', 'ours' and 'ourselves'.

So the bigger the photo, these professors argued, the greater the leader's arrogance and the more likely it was that their employees would feel alienated and undervalued, therefore undermining any sense of collective responsibility and endeavour. The leader would also be guilty of incubating other forms of dysfunctionality within their organisation. In short, '…this leadership style – let us call it narcissistic leadership – signals danger'.

© The Author(s) 2020
M. Cox, *The Business Case for Love*, https://doi.org/10.1007/978-3-030-36426-7_4

Wow, I remember thinking as we descended into Stockholm. Syed's inspired piece of journalism linked across sectors and organisations to highlight the danger of narcissistic leadership. He was proved right too. Within a year of the article's publication Mourinho was out.

The command and control approach to leadership is another, perhaps less colourful, way to describe what happened at Enron and at Manchester United. In the last century it was almost standard business practice throughout the world. Leaders were expected to be authoritative in nature and used a top-down approach, with privilege and power vested in senior management and with a clear gap between executives and workers. The BBC series 'Back in Time for the Factory' brought this to life when recreating the working condi-tions of a group of female factory workers in 1976. To the soundtrack of music from that year, it recreated the fight of these 'factory girls' for equal pay and highlighted just how much people's working lives existed in the com-mand and control culture prevalent at the time.

Much has changed in the 43 years since, yet remarkably the command and control approach to leadership still exists despite being at complete odds with the desires of today's employees. I have been lucky enough to work with hun-dreds of people over the last decade drawn from a variety of countries and cultures in the UK, Europe and beyond. Having listened to what they say and feel about being at work, my own experience suggests that for the vast major-ity of employees and in particular those under forty, expectations have changed significantly. How they see themselves at work and the behaviour they hope to see from their boss. They want their leaders to have clarity on, and com-municate openly, the direction of travel for the company, the financial objec-tives and the strategy to get there. They want this shared in an honest way. They also want to feel involved in bringing this strategy to life. They want to feel that they are collaborating with their peers and their leaders to get there.

I call this the 'Facebook' effect. The positive side of Facebook. Over the past 15 years people have become accustomed to a world of 'liking', 'commenting' and 'adding' to what they see on their social media feeds. They now want to do that at work. For them, there is a complete blurring of the lines, a mash-up of 'work' and 'play'. 'At work' no longer means 'being in the office'; 'at play' no longer means 'out of the office'. Technology means that today's employees dip into both on the way to work, while at work and on the way home. People no longer feel the need or desire to dress differently for work. Their 'work face' and their 'home face' are less distinct. Whilst they want to respect their lead-ers, they do not feel the need to hold them in reverence or want to be fearful in their presence. They expect similar levels of treatment and respect from their boss or colleagues that they have from their friends. They want to work with people they care about. They reject the old 'JFDI' (Just f****** do it), seeking instead a leadership approach and culture more in keeping with their needs and their own values.

So why does this outdated style of leadership still exist? Partly because most companies are still run by middle-aged-to-old white men, who were brought up in the old command and control style of business and therefore it is the only form of behaviour they have been exposed to. Partly because the skills needed to create a culture of collaboration and engagement with their employees are simply beyond them. They are not good listeners, and struggle with empathy. They see leadership through the prism of telling rather than sharing. They operate solely with the 'Head' and lead their company in a process-, operational-driven capacity focussed on the delivery of the numbers rather than how are we going to work together to make the numbers.

The huge down side of a command and control culture is that it breeds a lack of employee engagement, and more likely, a miserable employee experience. According to Gallup,[2] a staggering 87% of employees worldwide are not engaged, yet the benefit of highly engaged workforces is normally 'more money in the till'. Gallup estimate that this translates to a 10% higher customer metric, 17% higher productivity, 20% higher sales and 21% higher profitability. If people are not engaged or they are having a miserable time they stop caring. If they stop caring they are prone to make mistakes.

Which brings me to 'but I have an MBA!' Which of course, I don't. Let me be clear from the outset. I have nothing against the idea of further education and people investing in themselves for whatever reason they choose. This would be completely hypocritical, given that my son, Oliver, has a doctorate in history from the University of Oxford and my daughter, Sophie, has recently completed her Masters in Secondary Education at the Australian Catholic University in Sydney. My belief is that the skills, attitude and behaviours needed to be a successful leader have changed dramatically since 2008. So my question is: Have the business schools that promote the MBAs adapted to the new normal?

The 'pitch' from almost every business school could be paraphrased as 'in return for a lot of money that you pay us, we'll equip with you with the skills needed to earn more money than your peers'. Fine, but is that helping people become better leaders and allowing them to meet the needs and wants of today's employees. In 2018 the *Harvard Business Review* published a ranking of the best-performing CEOs in the world in 2017,[3] based essentially on the long-term success for the company they ran. Only 1 out of the top 10 had an MBA. That person was Sir Martin Sorrell, who resigned earlier in 2018 after a board-level investigation into his personal conduct and use of company money. The 2018 ranking again showed only 1 out of the top 10 had an MBA. This time it was Francois-Henri Pinault.[4] The year's top performer was Pablo Isla of Indetex, the parent of the retail fashion chains Zara, PullBear, Massimo Duto, Bershka, Stradivarius, Oysho, Uterque and Zara Home. What singled him out was a combination of humbleness and openness. Perfecting the art of management by walking around rather than the formality of meetings. Both Pablo Isla and Sir Martin Sorrell were also in the top 3 of the 2016 list, joined that year by Lars Rieben Sorensen of Novo Nordisk. In August of that year *Harvard Business Review*[5] hosted a roundtable with the three of them.

One topic was about corporate culture and leadership style. Pablo Isla commented

> In managing a company, you of course need to be rational. I lead a company with more than 150,000 employees and millions of customers. But I am gradually learning to be less rational and more emotional. Motivating people and generating a sense of spirit inside a company are essential parts of the CEO's role. We need to appeal to our employee's emotions to help create an environment when they can operate.

Sorensen added, 'For me, it's been a phenomenal journey. I've worked for this company for 34 years. I used to be an operational leader. But I've had to transform myself, to go from being very good at what I was doing technically, with domain expertise, to being a generalist – and then constantly being challenged'.

Other than the opportunity to earn more money, what are the skills that MBA graduates possess once they have handed over all those fees? Perhaps not surprisingly this varies according to the Business School's ethos and the curriculum. Most suggest a balance between 'head' and 'heart' skills. Problem solving, strategic thinking and planning, through to teamwork, communication and leadership.

I think something must be going wrong, as the reality is that the skills MBA graduates actually leave with seem somewhat different to those promised. In 2018 the *Financial Times* ran an article based on a survey of what employees actually want from an MBA graduate, highlighting that one in three of the employers surveyed said they struggled to find business school graduates with the right skills. The five most important skills were not MBA subjects, such as finance and marketing, but more loosely defined qualities, or so-called soft skills, such as the ability to work with a wide variety of people (cited by 76% of employers) and the ability to prioritise (cited by 72%).[6] In a more recent survey just under half of 72 employers said that they still struggled to find MBA graduates with the right mix of skills.[7] These are significant gaps and suggest either that Business Schools are not listening to the needs of Business or that they are not picking up on the broader trends of what people now expect from their experience of work.

At a time when employees are craving engagement and collaboration with their bosses, business schools are churning out MBA graduates who can read a finance report but struggle to 'read the room'. They are good on numbers but poor at empathy. The logical extension of this is that many companies remain reliant on their executives, armed with their MBAs as a badge of honour, who are taught all about profit but not about people. They are provided with a skill set more appropriate to last century, not this. How to 'hit the numbers' remains the dominant doctrine.

Perhaps these MBA courses would be better if they adopted two phrases I hear a lot when I am over in Scandinavia: 'Stomach Feeling' and 'Curiosity'. The former is self-explanatory and is about trusting one's instincts. The latter means being open-minded. Open to new ways of thinking. Open to fresh insights and perspectives. 'Leaning forward' into the conversation. Adopting a philosophy of 'Being Out: Not In' whereby most of the time they are away from their desks. Meeting their teams, meeting new people, embracing new ideas and cultures. Gaining insights which they will then take back to their own company.

'Being Curious' is, of course, neither a new behaviour nor exclusively Scandinavian. As the *Harvard Business Review*[8] noted a couple of years ago: 'Decades ago, Walt Disney declared that his company managed to keep innovating "because we are curious and curiosity keeps leading us down new paths"'. In the same article, when asked to name the one attribute CEOs will need most to succeed in the turbulent times ahead, Michael Dell, Dell Chief Executive, replied, 'I would place my bet on curiosity'.

Which brings us back to the MBA. Today's most successful leaders recognise the need to be 'heart led' not 'head led' and they understand the fundamental need to create empathy and a team spirit at work. But can this be taught? Can those who follow the doctrine of 'I' ever become converts to 'we'? Can those who believe business is only about profit and not people learn to think differently? Could Mrs. May have become less 'Maybot' and more empathetic? Perhaps, thankfully, we will never find out.

In the end this boils down to personal values and goals and what type of leader people see themselves as. Is their overriding focus on themselves? Are they driven largely by the goal of earning as much money for themselves as possible and not really bothered about the consequences? Or are they first and foremost about the team and wanting to build something exciting and sustainable and, of course, earning some money on the way? As Steve Jobs quite eloquently put it, 'Being the richest man in the cemetery doesn't matter to me. Going to bed at night saying we've done something wonderful, that's what matters to me'.[9]

This is a sentiment that was certainly not shared by Kenneth Lay and Jeffrey Skilling. Their narcissistic approach to leadership was part of their undoing. Both were convicted for their role in the collapse of Enron. Lay died before starting his sentence and Skilling has recently been released after having served 12 years.

Some people can and do change. Not everyone is born a leader. People can and do evolve their leadership skills, but only with the right mindset. They have to be curious, be comfortable in their own skin and believe in 'we' not 'I'. These are the building blocks for successful leadership given the new normal that we are now living in. Yet, sadly, these are three attributes that are often missing in many who have led and are still leading companies today. These are the attributes missing in the much-vaunted MBA education. This has disastrous results for the employee experience, the customer experience and ultimately the success of the business they are leading.

Notes

1. Syed, Matthew, 'Narcissistic leader Jose Mourinho out of touch with millennial footballers', *The Times*, 21 March 2019, https://www.thetimes.co.uk/article/narcissistic-leader-jose-mourinho-out-of-touch-with-millennial-footballers-t3kgd3zj0
2. 'Our approach to employee engagement is not working', Forbes, 30 September 2018, https://www.forbes.com/sites/nazbeheshti/2018/09/30/our-approach-to-employee-engagement-is-not-working/
3. 'The Best-Performing CEO's in the World 2017', *Harvard Business Review*, November–December 2017 issue, https://hbr.org/2017/11/the-best-performing-ceos-in-the-world-2017
4. 'The Best-Performing CEO's in the World 2018', *Harvest Business Review*, November–December 2018, issue https://hbr.org/2018/11/the-best-performing-ceos-in-the-world-2018
5. 'The Best-Performing CEO's in the World', *Harvard Business Review*, November 2016 issue, https://hbr.org/2016/11/the-best-performing-ceos-in-the-world

6. 'What employers want from MBA graduates-and what they don't', *The Financial Times,* 31 August 2017, https://www.ft.com/content/3c380c00-80fc-11e7-94e2-c5b903247afd

7. 'What top employers want from MBA graduates', *The Financial Times,* 3 September 2018, https://www.ft.com/content/64b19e8e-aaa5-11e8-89a1-e5de165fa619

8. 'Why Curious People Are Destined for the C-suite', *Harvard Business Review,* 11 September 2015, https://hbr.org/2015/09/why-curious-people-are-destined-for-the-c-suite

9. 'Steve Jobs quotes', Goodreads, https://www.goodreads.com/quotes/445606-being-the-richest-man-in-the-cemetery-doesn-t-matter-to

5

Fool's Gold

Back in my 'Mad Men' days, British Airways was known for producing memorable advertising, peaking with the 'Face' commercial in 1989 made by Saatchi and Saatchi, written by Graham Fink and Jeremy Clarke, and directed by Hugh Hudson.

It was created at a time when the airline called itself 'The World's Favourite Airline' based on the fact that it carried more international passengers than any other airline. Aside from its strong visual impact, the beauty of the ad was that it focused on what airlines are fundamentally about: bringing people together. Anyone working for British Airways could not help being proud of the airline they worked for. As a Brit I was also proud, and it was the airline of choice. 'To fly, to serve' sat proudly under its coat of arms. Thirty years on from 'The Face', 'To fly, to serve' remains, but the pride has gone, along with the claim to be the 'World's Favourite Airline'.

It now seems to be on a race to the bottom. Better known for 'To fly, to serve M&S sandwiches' and I hate what it has become. It represents what happens when the only goal seems to be a financial one and where the employee experience and the customer experience count for nothing. It's personal. For many years I was a Gold Card holder and now, unless the alternative is even worse, I refuse to fly with them. How sad is that?

Under the leadership of Willie Walsh and his sidekick Alex Cruz the airline is a mere shadow of its former self. They seem to personify the old-school command and control type of leadership discussed in the previous chapter. There was no one single incident that turned me from being a fan but rather a combination of experiences which ultimately added up to the feeling of: Why should I spend any more money with British Airways?

© The Author(s) 2020
M. Cox, *The Business Case for Love*, https://doi.org/10.1007/978-3-030-36426-7_5

Here is just one example amongst many. When I went to Japan, my wife Karen, son Oliver and I flew to see our then skiing instructor daughter Sophie who was working the season over there. We flew out British Airways and back on JAL. Same price. Both times Premium Economy. Two totally different experiences. With British Airways, an old plane, poor food and an in-flight crew going through the motions, versus JAL who had a brand new plane, excellent food and in-flight crew proud of their airline and proud to serve.

I can't remember the last time someone working at British Airways really seemed to care. The pilots are, of course, still out of central casting, and the crew sometimes do their best, but even they seem to have had enough and are no longer in love with the company they work for. It can't be much fun when the stated viewpoint from Alex Cruz is 'We have cost cutting in our DNA. If we do not come up with a cost cutting idea every day we are not doing our job'.[1] Bravo! Except one thing. The roots of British Airways are around service not just price. The well-spoken pilots have now resorted to strike action and are quick to point out that although part of it is to do with money, it is also to do with the sense of drift and overall direction of the company.

The employee experience seems almost as miserable as my own customer experience. I am not the only one feeling aggrieved at what the airline has become. Trustpilot now rates the company 1 star.[2] Customer comments from the month of September 2019 include complaints about the complete lack of care. No customer support at all in the UK. No idea about Customer Service. Incredibly rude staff. Poor Excuse for an airline. I would give it 0 stars if I could. Words fail me. Terrible Experience etc. And that was just from the first page. Seventy-nine percent of 1980 reviews on Trustpilot were classed as average to bad, with the latter making up 67% of responses. Even I was amazed at the amount of venom coming from aggrieved passengers. SkyTrax have rated the airline in the past with no more than 3 stars.[3] Putting it on a par with Air Namibia, Donghai Airlines, Kenya Airways and Mongolian Airlines, to name a few. A long way from 'The World's Favourite Airline'.

What's worse is that Willie Walsh and Alex Cruz don't seem to care. This is despite the luggage meltdown in 2017, the customer data theft in September 2018, the regular IT issues and the striking pilots. All they are worried about is maximising profit. Their only goal is a financial one. Offering an increasingly poor product for the highest price they think they can get away with. History suggests that this is not a sustainable proposition. An appalling customer experience, ultimately, means no business. One day in the future, the tipping point will come and British Airways is likely to come tumbling down.

Perhaps Willie Walsh, Alex Cruz and their advisors are blind to what has happened when other companies have taken a similar approach. Many retail companies in the UK have really struggled in recent months. When Toys 'R' Us went into administration in the early spring of 2018, no one was surprised. I had not been into a Toys 'R' Us for over 10 years. It was ghastly then, so heaven knows what it was like before it went bust. 'It's a magical place. We're on our way there'. So went the old jingle. Except it wasn't. It's a toy shop (or was). Where was the fun? Where was the magic? Where was the inspiration? Where was the memorable customer experience for kids of today (and their parents)? Yes kids have changed and are tech savvy at a young age. But they still want to have fun. Weighed down by debt, this was a failure of leadership, not a failure of the business environment. Where was the innovation? Where was the sense of 'being constantly inside the heads of the customer'? Which is a behaviour I will return to in future chapters. Were they listening and adapting to changing needs? Where was the service? Where was the product knowledge? Where was the bravery? Where was the Vision? If it can happen to Toys 'R' Us, it can happen to British Airways.

Mothercare and WH Smith are still going. Just. Although Mothercare's UK business has now closed. Both are victims of what happens when a company forgets what it stands for and what makes it different. Both are focussed on price points and promotions to survive. But it didn't have to be like this. Both were much-loved brands. Both have strong roots. Mothercare was founded by Iraqi-born entrepreneur Selim Zikha whose guiding principles were wonderful product design, knowledgeable staff and a fantastic customer experience. Caring for Mothers. Mothercare for short. It's in the name. Yet it stopped doing this. Seventy-six percent of customers on Trustpilot rated the experience as poor or bad (although admittedly from a tiny sample of just 21).[4]

This frustrates me as I had a close affiliation with the company as after my advertising days were over, I worked as a senior marketeer for BHS.

Mothercare was part of the Storehouse Group, as was BHS. The chairman was Sir Terence Conran, who had founded Habitat and was much loved by the City of London; he was seen as the person to re-energise tired and faded retail companies. Not long after, Mothercare was in the process of being transformed by the American CEO, Ann Iverson, previously Stores Director at BHS and who also holds the distinction of being the most terrifying person I have ever worked with! Nicknamed Cruella De Vil amongst her store team but I doubt ever to her face. Scary she might have been yet she and her team seemed to intuitively understand what was needed at Mothercare. They understood that Mothercare shoppers fell into two camps. Nervous first-time mothers who were looking for help, calm and reassurance. And more experienced mothers with perhaps more than one child and who desperately needed their children to be entertained/distracted whilst they shopped.

A completely new store design and environment was developed which included the 'Talking Trees' aimed at keeping young children amused and entertained. In contrast, pregnant mums had their own calmer part of the store where they could seek advice. These two different experiences were all about knowing the customer. Being curious, listening and understanding their needs. Then having the confidence and vision to create a memorable customer experience. And Ann never lacked in confidence. Ann then left the company for a not particularly successful stint as CEO of Laura Ashley and almost as soon as she was out of the door, the investment in the customer experience at Mothercare ceased, never to return.

Back over at WH Smith, and this year, once again, it has been voted the UK's worst-rated retailer in the recent Which? survey. The current Trustpilot score is 82% either bad or poor, with the former making up 75% out of a total of 467 reviews.[5] Described by *The Spectator* as a 'national embarrassment',[6] a visit to a WH Smith store is a bit like a trip to the dentist. Something to be endured rather than loved. Although at least with the dentist they stop short of trying to flog you chocolate when you come to pay.

It is the epitome of the transactional experience. I go (rarely), I buy (sometimes), I leave. I have no emotional relationship with the experience other than a mixture of anger and sadness. Similar to British Airways, the leadership team don't seem to care. It has reported a dip in profits, with high street trading down 6%[7] and overall group pre-tax profits down by 1%. The travel stores located in airports, railway stations and motorway services did well, with profits up by 5%. Where there is no competition and the customer is forced to go there, WH Smith is doing ok. Unlike on the high street where customers have a choice. That seems to be the strategy.

Talking of airports, what really bugs me is that the self-scanners at the airport continued to demand boarding passes from passengers two years after the VAT scam was exposed. Another area where customers are forced to use WH Smith is in hospitals where earlier in 2018 it was discovered that a Colgate toothpaste was being sold for £7.99 rather than the normal price of £1. They did apologise for that. Unlike the VAT scam.[8]

Once again a short-term cost-cutting strategy and a race to the bottom for a once great British company. It does not have to be like this and for a long time it wasn't. WH Smith was founded back in 1792 and for most of its life it represented all that was best in retailing. Innovative, not iterative, with the customer experience at the heart of the business. As late as 1995, it took the first secure online order on 27 April, which is recognised as the start of online shopping in the UK. How amazing is that! It was trusted and even 'loved', not least by budding authors who saw the company as a way to market their work.

What went wrong? Somewhere along the line the bosses seem to have lost sight of the importance of the employee and customer experience and just stopped investing. In the infrastructure and its people. Can you imagine what it must be like to work in a WH Smith store? Flogging chocolate all day at the till with, I would imagine, 99% of customers not wanting any? And as for those ghastly self-service machines… without a doubt the worst I know. They have certainly lost sight of what makes them different. Yet can you believe their stated values are:

- Customer Focus. Keep the customer at the heart of all that we do
- Value our People. Our people are respected and valued in an honest, open environment
- Drive for Results. Tenacity for ambitious and competitive results-driven with pace
- Accountability. Take personal responsibility and deliver what we say we will.

Yes, I am serious. Look it up online.[9] This is what makes me angry. A company that really does say one thing and do another. Remember those values if you ever visit a WH Smith store. Or battle with not showing your boarding card at the airport. Even more, tweet your experiences to WHS_Carpet (the twitter account for all things miserable about WH Smith). Britain's worst retailer? Probably. Given that most rivals for the title are now no longer trading.

The BHS I knew was very different to the one that went bust. My first direct experience of working with BHS was when I was the 'Account Man' for the business during the second half of the 1980s. As mentioned before, BHS became part of Storehouse plc with designer Sir Terence Conran at the helm. An early forerunner to Sir Richard Branson, this was a man who seemed to be single-handedly trying to improve the UK through offering better design. He had founded Habitat, written several design books (no self-respecting 'yuppie' home would be without one) as well as launching his own restaurants. He was part of the movement which became known as 'Cool Britannia'.

I have two very distinct memories of him, both of which are uncomfortable. For those who do not remember these days, BHS was a dowdy and frumpy competitor to the still mighty Marks & Spencer. At his heart, Conran was a product man and believed he could improve the company's image and fortunes through design, one product at a time. Not a million miles from the approach of Steve Jobs, except with BHS there were hundreds if not thousands of products to improve. I remember joining a 'product sign-off' meeting where Sir Terence Conran walked around with his coterie of directors like some latter-day Louis XVI of France acting as judge and jury as each person present explained and then defended the choice of products they wanted to put into stores. At some point he took a dislike to a range of bathroom accessories for the toilet (fluffy toilet roll holder, seat covers and rugs in a hideous pink) and simply exploded in disbelief at how awful they were…and he was right… leaving whoever was responsible in tears.

If he hated poor design he also had a universal dislike of advertising and admen. My agency was down to present that year's Christmas campaign which just happened to be the morning after the Great Storm of 1987. My Managing Director (MD) made it to the meeting, as did I, but the Creative Director could not, which meant it was down to me to present the campaign, which I duly did to the MD. Sir Terence Conran sat in the corner with his back turned to proceedings, displaying a complete lack of interest. Which for me was a probably a let-off.

No one could accuse the BHS team of not trying, and in 1989 they hired American David Dworkin who had been a former executive at Neiman Marcus to become CEO, and it was not too long afterwards that I joined to work for Marketing Director Helena Packshaw. My role was to update the image of the company, principally through advertising. I found David Dworkin quite remarkable as he was one of the first people I had come across who was a visionary and detail-obsessed at the same time. To have the guts to get BHS to be the first store to really try to own Christmas through its dedicated Christmas Shop whilst worrying about how many Pez sweets had been sold the day before.

Nearly 25 years or so after I left, BHS was in a sorry state. Just after it had entered administration, I visited the York store as I have had a soft spot for this store ever since facilitating some local marketing activity together with the York Tourist Board (for which I got roundly told off by my boss for not being clear about the expected ROI). What made me indignant was the condition of the store. It was abundantly clear that not a penny had been spent on it since my first visit. To be blunt, it was a mess, as of course became the company, the pension fund and the lives of the employees when it finally went bust.

Sir Philip Green will forever be associated with the collapse. He is apparently what everybody says he is. Now outed publicly for what was suspected privately.[10] Extremely rich and fully subscribed to the school of 'I' not 'we'. Seemingly focussed absolutely on the money and the deal with little sign of any love for his customers or his employees. He did pay £363 million into the BHS pension fund to help the shortfall which as *The Guardian* noted was likely to help him keep his knighthood.[11]

'Fool's Gold?'

Not for the bosses of British Airways, Mothercare, WH Smith and BHS. They have all done very well; other than Dominic Chappell, the last man standing at BHS and who no doubt will regret to his dying day trying to take on Sir Philip Green at his own game. Not for customers, who ultimately get fed up with the experience and stop spending money with the company.

Those who do suffer from 'Fool's Gold' are the employees. The everyday employees who listen to the speeches and see the PowerPoints from their bosses at the Company Meeting and the promise of a better tomorrow if you 'Just f****** well do it'. These are the ones where the treasure trove of wanting to feel pride in their company, feeling involved and happy in their work and fairly rewarded turns out to be worthless.

So, who or what kills the Company Spirit?

There are two forces at play. The behaviour of the boss and the consequential company culture together with the world we live in. Once separate but now entwined and connected.

When I started work, Margaret Thatcher had just come to power. The UK was starting to go through the type of change which turned out to be seismic: good for some and bad for others depending largely on what work you did and where you lived. Living in London I was aware of what was going on, but what was happening on the outside felt completely unconnected to my expectations of work.

Today, 10 years on from the Financial Crash we stand at a cross-roads. In fact, several almighty ones. Business and how we think and relate to business stands at one too. It only has itself to blame. Too often it appears on the front pages of our media for the wrong reasons. Scandal after scandal. Lies and deceit. 'Greed is Good'. The bankers got away with it. The Establishment got away with it. Trust remains broken. In the UK, people now question business and capitalism to such an extent that Jeremy Corbyn's pledge, as leader of the UK Labour Party, to re-nationalise large parts of the economy is hugely popular, particular with those under 40.

All of this has led many to question what we used to call the fabric of our society. The common thread that binds our interrelationships, be it personal, business or economic, has become frayed for many and broken for some. So if we do not trust what is happening on the outside, trust in our family, loved ones and the work we do becomes ever more important. We are human. We want to love and be loved so our expectations of what we want from 'going to work' have changed. Understanding and embracing this change is the challenge of today's leadership.

Companies that are loved by their customers are dynamic, resilient and successful. They believe in 'The Business Case for Love' and know how to bring it to life. They know it starts on the inside with employees loving their company for its values, sense of purpose and beliefs. They work hard to create trust, nurture curiosity, and protect the culture and company spirit this creates. This energy and belief drives the business and everything it does. Everything that the customer sees, feels and experiences is rooted in the Company Spirit.

Few leaders understand 'The Business Case for Love'.

Most view business as a game with no personal accountability, and care little about the consequences for the organisation. They are too often narcissists driven solely by personal gain: armed with their MBAs as their badge of honour. They understand business as a machine solely to create products and 'money in the till'. Heartless and mechanistic. Happy to create a purely transactional experience for employees and customers alike. They have no idea how to create companies that are loved by their employees, customers, the media and other stakeholders. These are the ones who kill the Company Spirit.

Companies that are thriving and not just surviving simply go another way. They view business as a social system operated by people for people. They care. They know that sustainable success or failure depends on the quality of relationships both inside and outside the company. They want to be the brand you brag about to your friends. They want you to love them.

Building a strong company spirit based on love requires a revolutionary philosophy and leadership style. The blinkers need to come off and a new wave of thinking embraced. Those who are stuck in their ways will find this a challenge. Those who are curious and seeking fresh insights and perspectives will feel invigorated.

Notes

1. 'Devotion to cost-cutting "in the DNA" at British Airways', *The Telegraph*, 29 May 2017, https://www.telegraph.co.uk/business/2017/05/29/devotion-cost-cutting-dna-british-airways/
2. 'British Airways', Trustpilot, September 2019, https://uk.trustpilot.com/review/www.britishairways.com
3. 'British Airways to Lose 4 Star Skytrax Rating-Rating It the Same as Ryanair!!!' *InsideFlyer*, 15 June 2017, https://insideflyer.co.uk/2017/06/british-airways-lose-4-star-skytrax-rating-rating-ryanair/

4. 'Mothercare', Trustpilot, September 2019, https://uk.trustpilot.com/review/mothercare.ie

5. 'WH Smith', Trustpilot, September 2019, https://uk.trustpilot.com/review/www.whsmith.co.uk

6. 'WH Smith has become a national embarrassment', *Spectator Life*, 14 December 2016, https://life.spectator.co.uk/articles/wh-smith-become-national-embarrassment/

7. 'WH Smith posts 6% fall in high street profits', *Retail Gazette,* 12 April 2018, https://www.retailgazette.co.uk/blog/2018/04/whsmith-posts-6-fall-high-street-profits/

8. 'WH Smith apologises after selling toothpaste for £7.99 in a hospital', *i News*, 11 May 2018, https://inews.co.uk/news/uk/wh-smith-toothpaste-hospital-511041

9. 'About Us. WH Smith', http://www.whsmithcareers.co.uk/about-us/

10. 'Sir Philip Green named as man at heart of "UK #metoo scandal"', *The Guardian*, 26 October 2018, https://www.theguardian.com/world/2018/oct/25/sir-philip-green-named-as-man-at-centre-of-uk-metoo-scandal

11. 'Philip Green agrees to pay £363 m into BHS Pension Fund', *The Guardian*, 28 February 2017, https://www.theguardian.com/business/2017/feb/28/philip-green-agrees-pay-363m-bhs-pension-fund

Part II

Falling in Love

6

Becoming Bragged About

How a company gets bragged about has changed enormously over the last 30 years. During my career in Advertising and my relatively brief sojourn in Marketing the main tool a company used to get talked about was in fact advertising. Back then and when used correctly it really could change how we thought about a company or a brand. Perhaps most famously during this period was the Launderette commercial made for Levi's 501 jeans by Bartle Bogle and Hegarty in 1985. Sales of 501s, which were seen as unfashionable and not even something your dad would wear, increased by 800%, boxer shorts were reborn, and Nick Kamen who had the main role in the commercial briefly became a star in his own right. The music, Marvin Gaye's 'I Heard It Through the Grapevine' was re-released and made it into the top 10. It was one of the most talked about campaigns of the decade. Most clients then expected their agency to be able to do a 'Levi's'. A few years later, BHS was no exception.

My own time working at BHS was not a particularly happy one. Indeed, I was fired. Maybe not fired as such. More let go. David Dworkin had left for pastures new to be replaced by someone who I did not like and did not rate. The feeling was clearly mutual. For a while I reverted to being a consultant to my old boss and continued to advise on the development of the advertising campaign. I had found it was not easy to go from an agency to working on the client side. In truth I realised how little I knew about business other than how to do advertising. It didn't help that very few (maybe two or three people out of thousands) at BHS understood the role of advertising and marketing. Most people saw marketing as a cost and we were seen as the people 'who did the signs or the posters for the windows'.

© The Author(s) 2020
M. Cox, *The Business Case for Love*, https://doi.org/10.1007/978-3-030-36426-7_6

During my time there we had hired what was seen as the most innovative agency of the period, HHCL, to help do a 'Levi's' and change how people thought about the company. They created a campaign for BHS which was brave but very polarising. A 'Marmite' campaign, or 'Vegemite' if reading this down under. It very much split opinion. The new CEO hated it, which didn't help my cause.

The advertising business at this time was a relatively simple affair. There was what was called 'above the line' (commercials etc.) and 'below the line' (direct mail etc.). Ad agencies only really focussed on the former whilst looking down their noses at the latter. 'Posh Brands' would appear during the centre break of 'News at Ten' whilst 'Family Brands' would appear during the centre break of 'Coronation Street'. Creating successful campaigns which would get the company bragged about did happen, although not all the time. London had some of the best, brightest and most creative talent in the world, and some of the advertising created during this period was, and remains, on a par with the very best. My wife, Karen, was a media planner at Collett Dickenson Pearce, which was regarded as Britain's most glamorous and influential agency. Indeed, many thought it to be the finest creative agency in the world. 'Happiness is a cigar called Hamlet', 'Land Rover. The best 4 X 4 X Far' and perhaps most famous of all "Heineken refreshes the parts other beers cannot reach" became national institutions rather than mere campaign slogans. Ads for Hovis and Cinzano were equally famous. Directed by Ridley Scott, who went onto direct *Blade Runner*, *Alien* and *Gladiator*, and Alan Parker respectively. *Chariots of Fire* director Hugh Hudson also worked there. It is fair to say the agency knew how to get their clients' brands bragged about.

HHCL had some of the best minds working for it, something I had come to appreciate when working at BBDO. It was here I had the great pleasure of working with one of the stand-out planners, Kay Scorah. Planning, as a discipline, was relatively new at this time and Kay had been at the vanguard of its development. It was essentially about talking to people in order to gain insights so that the advertising duly created was based on a message both compelling and true. John Hegarty's book *Turning Intelligence Into Magic*[1] is a brilliant read capturing some of the best moments from those times and highlights the link between planning, 'the intelligence' and the creative work 'the magic'. He also happened to be the creative director responsible for Levi's.

There was also many a campaign from those times where the magic failed to happen, mainly because the image portrayed bore little resemblance to the actual product, and certainly not the customer or employee experience. So, despite the clever thinkers involved, this is what happened with the BHS campaign. It was nobly trying to get people to think differently about the company, yet in reality was a million miles away from what customers found in the stores, or the experience of those employees who worked there. Despite some superhuman efforts, many products were still dowdy, and the actual shopping experience varied wildly depending on which store was visited. The advertising was creating a promise of a better tomorrow, which is what most campaigns from that time did. Tomorrow never really came and the image portrayed in the commercials and the experience of going to the store did not match. There was no 800% increase in sales.

Like some latter-day conversion of Saul to Paul, my BHS experience completely changed the way I thought. As opposed to trying to create change from the outside, I now believed the start point should be the other way around. From the inside. Or put another way, start internally with 'What does the company stand for?' not externally with 'What is the image we are trying to create?' There was no straight line from this conversion to writing this book but it was the seed which became the philosophy and approach I call the 'Business Case for Love'.

My other big learning from the BHS days was that in order to create change, people needed to feel involved in its creation, and not just have it imposed upon them. Quite simply, if people feel they have created something as a team they really believe in it and feel passionately about it. This is why, not surprisingly, an agency's creative team would defend their work to the nth degree. They had created it and they believed in it. Although the best creatives were always happy to listen, and take on board comments from myself or a client, if these points made sense. It was the less talented teams who would revert to the more aggressive tactics of 'Don't come back unless you've sold the ad!' So all in all, this was a time which shaped not only what I believed in, but what I set out to do.

Fast forward a few years and I was a partner at The Gathering. Founded by Duncan Bruce, the outputs were primarily brand identity, design and innovation. It was the way the company worked with its clients which provided a stepping stone to my current philosophy. There was never a dull moment working with Duncan, as he was somewhat mercurial in character. In many ways, we could not have been more different, yet for a brief few years we came together as the 'odd couple' with me playing the straight man to Duncan's creative virtuosity. The core of our work together was to help a brand team gain clarity on what it stood for and what made it different. Duncan's view was the clearer the team in their thinking, the better the brief and the better the resultant creative work, and he was right. The way we did this was to put a team through a series of experiences, normally over a couple of days, which would allow me to facilitate those involved in creating what we called the

Brand Spirit. This way of working helped me bring to life the principal learnings from my BHS days. Namely it was an 'inside out' way of working and it created huge ownership amongst the team because they had created, with a little help, their Brand Spirit and therefore really owned it.

Our work together took us to many parts of the world and we helped a number of brands. Two projects in particular helped evolve my own thinking: the snack brand Estrella in the Nordics and Robert Bosch in Germany, the USA and the UK. With both, although there was a creative output, the principal impact of the work was on how people started to behave. As a consequence I started to become much more interested in the link between company values and behaviours rather than brand communication. A few years later I founded The Company Spirit.

My focus now is company culture, and I get hired to 'kick off' behavioural change. To help create the mindset of memorable employee experiences, which lead to memorable customer experiences and sustainable commercial success. Get that right and the company starts to get bragged about. The way I go about this is rooted in my advertising, BHS and The Gathering experiences.

Today the 'signature dish' of my work is to bring a group together. Normally for two days, to help facilitate the creation of their Company Spirit. Before arriving people are always set a little light homework, namely to 'think about a customer experience they love and be prepared to share why. This can be anything from a global brand, to your favourite restaurant or sports team. The important part is that you have an emotional and loyal relationship with your choice'.

I do this for two main reasons. It makes people think a little about their own experiences as a customer, and it then allows me to use these insights at the very beginning of my 'Company Spirit Events'. To start to help people think differently.

I've developed some of my own techniques to allow people to have fresh insights and perspectives about the company they work for, and one of them is what I call 'Bringing The Outside In'. I've learnt the hard way that if I start an Event by asking people to talk about their own company it usually ends badly. They struggle to articulate what they feel in a clear and precise way and start to squabble amongst themselves about the rights and wrongs, and whose fault it is, which can add up to a negative, destructive atmosphere, with some in the room already starting to mentally check out.

Starting in a different way, and with them sharing their story about a 'customer experience I love', has a completely different effect. First, no one is wrong. It's their experience after all. So people relax and start to engage and listen to each member of the group when it is their turn. Second, when viewed from their own experience as a customer, people find it very easy to describe why they love the company involved. People have very strong opinions on what works for them, what does not and what goes wrong. Love, as in life, can turn to hate if the customer is betrayed.

Over the years, I have listened to hundreds of people answer this question so I have a pretty good idea about how a company needs to behave to be bragged about today. The big change is that virtually no one talks about their advertising! The companies mentioned may have changed over time but the reasons why have always been, and remain, remarkably consistent. What I love about listening to the comments is that it acts as a 'real-time' view of how people are feeling and how they think the company is doing. Sometimes people talk about a company that they still love, but have started to notice things that are beginning to niggle at them, and these insights can provide a great guide to the future performance of a company. Something small which at the time can seem quite incidental can often be a sign of 'trouble at t'mill' where those at the top have started to focus on just the numbers and not the customer experience.

One such incident is etched in my mind from almost 30 years ago. Once upon a time Marks & Spencer could do no wrong. The company, along with I.C.I was often talked about as a 'bellwether UK stock'. As my old boss at BHS used to say, '...it was the only store in the UK when you felt it was your fault if they had run out of what you wanted because you had got there to late'. If the company was doing well then the stock market was doing well. Marble Arch was the flagship store and held up as a beacon of success. In the early 1990s my wife and I were clothes shopping with our very young son in their children's department, which was in the basement. Not long after our arrival, young Oliver announced that he needed to go to the toilet and as any parent knows that means fast action is needed to avert any puddles. So I quickly found an assistant and asked where the customer toilets were and she said they didn't have any. Rather taken aback by this, I asked her what to do and she said go to Selfridges, the department store over the road. Somewhat baffled by the response, we duly did and with great haste.

Not too many years after this incident, profits peaked in the financial year 1997/1998 only to slump dramatically from a billion pounds in 1997 to £145 million in the year ended 31 March 2001.[2] The share price fell by more than two thirds. This took everyone at the company, in the City and in the media by surprise. All except the customers whose loyalty had been seriously eroded. For the previous few years the company had only focussed on the bottom line and not the customer experience. Trust was broken and love turned to annoyance, frustration and then hate. M&S has never really recovered from this.

So was there a connection between our toilet incident a few years earlier and M&S's sudden fall from grace? In my mind, absolutely. Growth had led to arrogance and not caring for their customers or, as it turned out, their employees. Are you listening Willie Walsh and Alex Cruz?

Another example of something small suggesting trouble ahead happened at Starbucks. The story of the breakfast sandwich is much more widely known, mainly because Howard Schultz, the original CEO, used it as an example in his highly readable book *Onward*. He tells of Starbucks' 'fight for life without losing its soul', having had its own M&S moment when everything came crashing down. It is the perfect example of what happens when the only focus is growth and people become blinded to what's really happening, because all the numbers seem to be pointing in the right direction.

Around the time of the millennium I was travelling to the Chicago area relatively frequently. There was a Starbucks across the road from the offices I was visiting and I would often pop in. The company at the time was in its pomp. Seemingly it could do no wrong, yet, in its quest for growth lay the seeds of its almost terminal collapse. In order to gain more dollars per visit it was starting to offer almost anything other than coffee, including the sale of CDs by Joni Mitchell and Paul McCartney at the counter. Starbucks had entered the music business and I remember thinking this felt a little odd.

During this time Howard Schultz had become Chairman and spent most of his time 'shaking hands at various store openings' but intuitively started to feel that there was something wrong at Starbucks, even though the numbers were fine. For Schultz it was not the music on sale but the smell of burnt cheese. 'People who have known me for years will tell you that few things had piqued my ire as much as that smell', Schultz wrote, 'I could not stand it'.[3] Having opposed the idea of selling breakfast sandwiches from the beginning, he hated the way 'singed Monterey Jack, mozzarella, and most offensively cheddar' from the sandwiches overwhelmed the aroma of coffee. 'Where was the magic in cheese?' he wrote, and added, 'The breakfast sandwich became my quintessential example of how we were losing our way'. Or put another way, in the search for growth, Starbucks forget to look after its core product: the coffee and its enticing aroma. Schultz went on to write, 'If not checked, success has a way of covering up small failures. This is why, I think, so many companies fail. Not because of challenges in the marketplace, but because of challenges on the inside'. A crucial lesson he learnt while tackling these challenges is one that is all too easy to ignore: 'Growth, we now know all too well, is not strategy. It is a tactic'.[4] Getting bragged about is great, as long as the company does not forget why it was loved in the first place.

There are some companies who have maintained bragging rights during the 10 years or so that I have been asking people to share their views on customer experiences or a company they love. Top of the pile is Apple. It almost always comes up. Wherever I am in the world. It is not without its faults though, and is prone to the occasional wobble. People are quick to point out when they think Apple has made a mistake. I remember a couple of newly employed graduates going apoplectic over the launch of the iPhone 5 and iPhone 5s as they felt it complicated the decision of what to buy rather than making it simpler. Nevertheless, it is the only global company, along with Amazon and to a lesser degree Google, which has been bragged about consistently over the years.

The country I am in makes a difference, with pride in a nation's companies to the fore. In Denmark, Lego is a favourite, which used to be joined by B&O but not anymore. In Sweden it's Volvo, although they reminisce about Saab, and they have a love/hate relationship with IKEA. In Finland it used to be Nokia but this has now been replaced by some obscure liquorice brand with, to a British ear, a baffling pronunciation. In Norway, Helly Hansen or Freia, the local chocolate brand. No one has a good word to say about SAS, the airline and Scandinavian flag carrier.

When in Texas, USA, something unique occurred. A lot of the men present talked about their love for the armed services. The Navy Seals, the Marines or the Green Berets. Either that or sports teams. Another first. People talked about a team that they did not necessarily support but they did admire. Akin to a Manchester United supporter praising the way Manchester City play.

My one time in Romania and it was like people were on a speed dial to catch up with 'western brands' and it was here that Pizza Hut made its one and only appearance.

Back in the UK, John Lewis and its supermarket offspring Waitrose would be regularly mentioned, although the last few years has seen a distinct cooling towards both of these. First Direct holds the distinction of being the only bank or financial service company to come anywhere near being loved. Ted Baker would pop up occasionally, although following allegations of misconduct by its founder, no more. M&S Food used to come up, but no longer. Not much love for the other supermarkets and never for the utilities or the telephone companies. The airlines are a category unto themselves. People are usually full of praise for the Middle Eastern and Far Eastern carriers. Virgin Atlantic every so often. There used to be a fair amount of love for Ryanair—'I know it's going to be crap but it didn't cost a lot and I'll have a great time when I get there'—but less so now. I am not the only one to despair about what British Airways has become.

There is, however, one long-term trend. People rejecting the big for the small. The return of the 'Independents', online and with a mix of channels where people felt that they were treated as an individual and not a number. A perfect example of these new wave companies is Cubitts, the London-based spectacle and sunglasses brand. Founded in the newly hip King's Cross in 2012 by Tom Broughton. This company first came to my attention through my wife ordering a home trial, having become disenchanted with the more transactional glasses brands. In her second career, as an interior designer, Karen has an eye for form and function and an attention to detail. So when her 'home trial' arrived the first thing she noticed was how beautifully packaged the frames were. Clearly having taken a leaf out of Apple, the positive first impression was the packaging. The frames themselves were beautifully designed and as we were later to find out made in a traditional way with a craftsman's touch. So began our love affair with Cubitts as the home trial took us to visit the stores where knowledgeable and quirky staff help you to buy a design that doesn't just look good but fits the face as well. Not the cheapest, but in our eyes very good value for money. So one purchase became two and within a year or so our extended family all became fans, which means I would imagine nearly 15 pairs of spectacles or sunglasses have been brought as a result of that first home trial, including a pair of my own sunglasses proudly worn by my daughter when she used to lifeguard on Coogee Beach, Sydney.

Speaking of brand loyalty, we now have a brilliant independent butcher in Gerrards Cross. Savanna Family Butchers is run by a South African duo, Davin and Cyreane Clement. It has a very loyal and growing following, because Davin is a first-rate butcher serving excellent quality meat who cares passionately about the provenance of what he is selling. Plus he has time to chat to everyone who comes into the shop, making the experience much more personal and fun. Davin was also quite brave in the location of his shop. Sited opposite Waitrose and close to Tesco because he believed he would be able to offer a better experience.

Having the time for a chat is a virtue that has remained paramount on the other side of the channel. France is probably Europe's strongest supporter of the independent store. No visit to the local boulangerie is complete without a quick catch-up on village gossip, and their food markets continue to thrive. Offering wonderful locally sourced produce, good value for money as well as the opportunity to improve my French.

These are a few of the hundreds of different companies mentioned to me over the years. All sorts of sizes and categories. Some big, some small. Some old, some new. Nowadays many more are just online or, like Cubitts, have worked out how the online and in-store experiences should be complementary ones for the customer, not competitive, with different parts of the same business seemingly trying to attract the customer's attention to buy through their channel only. Remarkably though, when asked to share how they thought a company behaved to create this sense of love, the thoughts of hundreds of people from all parts of the world have been greatly similar and consistent. They were and still are always a combination of 'heart' and 'head'. Emotional and rational reasons which when combined in the right way triggered a memorable customer experience. Looking back across all these comments and insights there are four standout behaviours which lead to a customer experience being seen as memorable and the company being bragged about:

- Simple and Consistent: a clear and simple idea based on a great product or service executed consistently over time;
- Personal and Individual: an experience that suggests these companies know their customers mindsets and work hard at being 'in the moment' to meet their needs;
- Emotional Connection: a belief in the ethos of the company that shines through with happy staff with terrific product knowledge living an authentic, honest culture based on genuine values;
- More than a transaction: a focus on the overall customer experience and not just a 'product at a price' mentality with the company clear and confident in what makes it different.

None of these four behaviours are particularly difficult to achieve. They do not cost a lot of money. They are all about having the right internal mindset and culture. Led from the top. The opposite behaviour to the fish rots from the head down.

Of course the tools to enable bragging to happen have changed somewhat since my BHS days. Social media has revolutionised the speed and scale of communication. Although to the casual observer, Twitter seems to attract those who have a complaint, and Instagram those who want to celebrate something good. This means that there is now no place to hide. Get it right and a reputation can soar. Get it wrong and it can crash and burn within days or even hours.

Notes

1. Hegarty, John. 'Hegarty on Advertising; Turning Intelligence into Magic', Thames & Hudson 2011.
2. Marks & Spencer Financial Decline, Wikipedia, https://en.wikipedia.org/wiki/Marks_%26_Spencer
3. 'How Starbucks got its groove back', *Fortune,* 24 March 2011, https://fortune.com/2011/03/24/how-starbucks-got-its-groove-back/
4. Schultz, Howard. 'How Starbucks Fought for Its Life without Losing Its Soul'. John Wiley & Sons 2011.

7

Love Is in the Air

During the life of The Company Spirit I have worked with clients in a wide range of categories. Automotive, Computer Software, Education, Engineering, Financial Services, FMCG, Government, Retail, Technology and Transport. Interestingly, there is one characteristic common to all of them. Every team gets obsessed with how they compare within their category and judge themselves solely against their immediate competition.

Sometimes this is understandable, and physical location can compound this behaviour. When I helped a team at Mercedes who worked in showrooms around the London area, their competition was quite literally next door. They would spend their days gazing out at the opposition, be it Audi, BMW or Jaguar. The temptation was to play the game of 'follow the leader' for fear of missing out. Metaphorically, if one dealer got the balloons out to highlight a sales event, everyone followed suit.

When I worked with Kraft in the Nordics, the benchmark would be P&G or Unilever, with all reviews based on how each company matched up against the other. Software companies would judge themselves against other software companies.

Retailers are the worst. Constantly popping into one another's shops, and the moment someone puts a promotion on, everyone reacts to do the same. Knowing what your competition are up to is good but if that's all a company does it creates a very narrow frame of reference. It breeds complacency, a lack of ambition and innovation.

Perhaps that is why so many customer experiences end up feeling the same.

Yet as customers we do not think like that. We walk around with this Rolodex of experiences in our head and judge what we see and what we feel

© The Author(s) 2020

M. Cox, *The Business Case for Love*, https://doi.org/10.1007/978-3-030-36426-7_7

against that. Sometimes these are subliminal, others may loom large, but they all exist within the vortex of our mind. So the experience we have with an airline will partly be influenced by other flights and other airlines, but could equally be influenced by the last visit to an Apple Store, the online chat with our broadband supplier, the service and quality of the food at a favourite restaurant or the last train journey we went on. We have this mental ranking system, and being human, we tend to score the experience we are currently having versus the best we remember. Even if we do not realise we are doing it. Companies that are thriving at the moment understand the importance of this. Which is why part of my philosophy and approach with my clients is to help them take the blinkers off and aspire to behave as a 'Best in Class' company, not just 'Best in Category'.

What does it take to behave as 'Best in Class'? Through a combination of my own personal experiences as a customer, observations about how winning companies behave and perhaps most importantly listening to the comments and opinions of the hundreds of people I have worked with, I have come to the conclusion that there are six 'Best in Class' company behaviours which really do separate the best from the rest. They live each of the six, and through doing so have a completely different mindset. One that results in love being in the air for their employees and customers. Let's explore each one in turn.

Ensuring Image and Experience Match

One of the biggest changes since my advertising days is that we now judge a company not just by what it says but also what it does. Yet I am amazed by how many companies still persist in focussing on the image they would like to project, and not thinking enough about the actual experience a customer has. United Airlines asked us to 'Fly the Friendly Skies', which first originated back in 1965 with a real-life Don Draper, the fictional creative director in 'Mad Men', coining the phrase to 'show the public our warm "good guy" genuine concern side, as well as the efficient side they already appreciate in us'.[1] Even without the Dr. Dao incident, I have flown enough flights with United to know that the image and the experience do not match. Functional maybe, but compassionate and friendly? This after all was the same airline which unwittingly became the star of the YouTube sensation 'United Breaks Guitars'.[2] Penned and starring Canadian Musician Dave Carroll as the only way he knew to get United to take notice of his claim for his guitar which had been broken by baggage handlers fooling around when on a stopover at Chicago O Hare International. After nine months of fruitless negotiations,

Carroll did what he did best and wrote a song to vent his frustration not just at the original breakage but the way he had been dealt with afterwards. First posted on 6 July, 2009, it amassed 150,000 views within one day, 500,000 views three days later and 5,000,000 by mid-August. At the time of writing there have been 19,532,097 views. United duly apologised and offered a belated compensation which did little to quell a massive public relations disaster which shone a light on the less than compassionate culture at United. The airline continued to ask its customers to 'Fly The Friendly Skies', and still did even after Dr., Dao walked on board some nine years later.

The banks of course are pass masters at saying one thing and doing another. Given there are so many examples to choose from, the question is where to start. The one that sticks in my memory most is UK bank NatWest and their 'Helpful Banking' campaign. In one way it was a good idea. The creation of a Customer Charter,[3] whereby the bank committed itself to a number of pledges to make life better for their customers. A campaign which was launched not long after the financial crash had left trust in UK banks at absolute rock bottom. No doubt some bright spark within the marketing team had uncovered the insight that banks are seen as in it for themselves and not on the side of the customer. The same bright spark thought 'but we just can't say that we need to show we mean it' and NatWest. Helpful Banking was born. I do not know this for certain but this idea smacks of the same mistake I made with BHS. It was an outside:in approach. This campaign could only work if NatWest really was helpful, which would have meant a significant change of culture and behaviour within the bank. The other flaw in this approach was that it left the bank open to huge criticism if something went wrong. Which in fact it did on frequent occasions. So at the same time the Customer Charter was promising some nice platitudes, years of underinvestment in the IT infrastructure resulted in the bank failing at the most basic task: to allow people access to their money and to be able to use their debit card. This happened first in 2012 and relatively frequently over the following six years. Every time it happens NatWest says 'Sorry' (that word again) but when they were still using Helpful Banking, the 'Sorry' would appear under the tagline NatWest. Helpful Banking.

Did anybody within the marketing team or their agency not think that this was completely nuts? Have our banks learned anything over the last 10 years? Apparently not, as shown by the events at TSB in 2018. Another bank, another IT meltdown, another shut-out for customers and another CEO saying sorry a lot. Christened the Totally Shambolic Bank,[4] TSB was, along with the CEO, Paul Pester, now the ex-CEO, guilty of saying one thing and doing another. Supposedly caring about their customers whilst doing an IT upgrade on the cheap.

Then there is Tesco and when the beef in the beef burger turned out to be horsemeat. I have never been a fan of Tesco for the way the company has consistently behaved down the years. I remember during my The Gathering years sitting in reception at their Cheshunt office and I could smell the fear. Decent suppliers knowing that they were about to be beaten down on price by the 'bully boy' buyers. A few years on and I was witness to another side of Tesco's character. I live in Gerrards Cross, in Buckinghamshire and to the west of London, and during the late 1990s Tesco brought the 'air' over the railway line in order to build a supermarket. On the evening of 30 June 2005 the tunnel which was being built over the railway line to create the foundations for the supermarket collapsed. Miraculously and despite it being rush hour no train was affected and therefore no injuries occurred. Those travelling by train that evening were incredibly lucky, and the consequent inconvenience of the line being out of action for a while was tiny compared to what could have happened. Various investigations have taken place, with the Health and Safety Executive launching one of their own, which remained open until 2015. A final report has been prepared which to this day has still not been made public pending resolution of legal issues.[5] The store went on to be opened in 2010 but to this day I have no recollection of Tesco ever saying sorry to the good people of Gerrards Cross. Probably the lawyers told them not to as that would have been seen as an admission of guilt.

So I was not surprised when the horse meat scandal broke in 2013. Tesco were not the only company involved but in the UK they took centre stage. This time Tesco did say sorry, whilst largely putting the blame on its suppliers. Back to my observation of the 'bully boy' buyers. If price becomes the dominant force in the relationship then a company can take desperate steps to keep the business. This appears to be what happened, with suppliers replacing beef with cheaper horse meat so they could reduce costs, hit their margins and keep their Tesco contact.

Neither was I surprised when the news broke in September 2014 that Tesco had overstated its profits by some £250 million for the first half of its financial year. The toxic culture I had witnessed came home to roost. This time there was a trial, with the prosecution opening the case by stating

the defendants were aware that income was being wrongly included in the financial records of the company which were used to inform statements to the stock market. They were aware that this was being done in order to meet targets so that the company would look financially healthier than it was. They were aware that this wrongly included income would result in Tesco's trading profit and share price being overstated.[6]

A sad footnote to this is that I knew one of the defendants when he was a junior brand manager at Kraft and found it hard to believe he really was standing in the dock. All three defendants were cleared, although much was made of the poor culture at Tesco during the trial.[7] Tesco remains an example of what can happen when the only thing people care about is hitting the numbers. When the image 'Every Little Helps' does not match the everyday experience for employees, suppliers and customers alike. This latest shock to the system seems to have been the catalyst for a change of behaviour led by Group CEO Dave Lewis who has recently announced he will leave his role in 2020. Time will tell whether what Tesco says and what it does ever become one and the same.

What I struggle with is understanding why a company still thinks that it is okay for their image and experience not to match. There is still a lot of brand communication I see, and I think to myself that it is just not the experience I have. Marketeers and agency people are not stupid. They know that in today's world one false step has the potential to be captured and then shared. This is the new paradigm. A company can no longer behave in a bad way and get away with it. It will be found out. It's just a question of when. The incident with Dr. Dao was captured on iPhone and went viral within a day or two. It took Dave Carroll nine months to resort to YouTube to finally make his point. Twitter storms flair up in an instant with every new banking IT fiasco.

Perhaps the answer is in the word 'Brand'. This word, along with 'Vision', is the most misunderstood and misused word in business. 'Brand' and 'Branding' are not the same thing. Yet so many CEOs confuse the two, and if they are confused, heaven help the rest of their company. Ask a CEO to talk about their Brand and many will then talk about their logo, the advertising, the design. This is 'Branding'. It is the image portrayed. The 'Brand' is what the company stands for. Its values, sense of purpose and beliefs. Summed up succinctly by Tony Hsieh, CEO of Zappos, in his book *Delivering Happiness: A Path to Profits, Passion and Purpose*, as 'Your Culture Is Your Brand' and 'Our belief is that a company's culture and a company's brand are just two sides of the same coin. The brand is just a lagging indicator of the culture',[8] as United, NatWest and Tesco all found out. Or as Jeff Bezos, founder and CEO of Amazon, is fond of saying, 'Your brand is what other people say when you're not in the room'.[9] Given their similar views, if expressed slightly differently, perhaps it is not a surprise that when Amazon acquired Zappos in 2009 a main priority for Hsieh and supported by Bezos was the preservation of the

Zappos culture so the image and experience continued to match. Say what you do and do what you say is a simple behaviour yet a major stepping stone to being bragged about for the right not the wrong reasons.

Being Constantly Inside the Heads of Customers

On 15 January 2013, HMV, once an icon on the British music scene, went into administration. The following weekend on 20 January, *The Sunday Times* ran an article headlined 'HMV deaf to internet threat'[10] and it described how 'as the internet changed the way we shop, HMV stopped listening to its customers and now the retailer has paid the price'. The article went on to be quite damning of the leadership team involved and claimed, quite rightly, that if they had a culture of listening to their highly knowledgeable customers they would have picked up years before that people were talking about 'streaming' and 'downloading', and responded accordingly. To know your customers. To be curious about them. To talk with them. To listen and understand what they are thinking. This can't be difficult, can it? Yet not listening is often the first thing a company does when it starts to lose its way.

Every founder, every start-up, every fledgling company will go out of its way to talk and listen to their customers. The challenge comes later on when a company grows and is successful, and this is the point where some stop behaving in the very way that helped them become successful in the first place. Some companies become arrogant, believing they can walk on water, thinking they can do no wrong. 'Pride comes before the fall' comes from the Book of Proverbs in the Bible. I actually prefer the original quote from the King James Bible of 'Pride goeth before destruction, and an haughty spirit before a fall'. Fred Goodwin comes to mind. So does Sir Richard Greenbury, the man at the helm of Marks & Spencer when it slumped in the late 1990s. He has only recently died and the obituaries pull no punches. To quote *The Guardian,* 'Greenbury was an autocratic and abrasive chairman. He led M&S to record success but failed to admit the need for change in a shifting fashion market, which precipitated a dramatic collapse in the company's fortunes'.[11] Previously, journalist Judi Bevan had laid bare the culture Greenbury created in her book *The Rise and Fall of Marks & Spencer,* summed up '...by how seniority of the directors was denoted by the depth of their carpets, the size of their desks and the number of their windows'.[12] Greenbury oversaw a culture with the leadership team loathing one another and an inability or desire to listen to their employees and customers. No wonder there were no customer toilets in the Marble Arch store then.

Contrast this with the behaviour of another retail titan, IKEA. As of June 2019, more than 900 million people in 52 countries visited its stores and it had sales in 2018 of more than 38 billion euros.[13] The IKEA website contains 12,000 products and there were over 2.1 billion visitors in a year (September 2015 to August 2016). Who said 'retail is dead'? Guided by the principle of creating 'a better everyday life for the many people' and the values of founder Ingvar Kamprad,[14] IKEA is a company that lives and breathes its unique company spirit creating a cult-like devotion in employees and customers alike (with the occasional 'hate' when stuck in the queue or lost in bedding). In February 2018, the BBC shone a light on this culture with a three-part series called 'Flatpack Empire'. I loved every minute of it, particularly because they demonstrated the absolute mindset of 'being inside the heads of their customers', not just to listen to what they say but to observe how people live. 'Be Out. Not In' is the rally call I give to my clients, and this is what the IKEA team do. Cameras followed Mia Lunstrom as she toured the markets of Hyderabad and visited people's homes as they prepared to launch in India. She has lived there for three years and the company have undertaken over 800 'home visits' to understand how people live and what people want from a home so IKEA can adapt accordingly. Back over in the UK and the cameras followed visual merchandiser Rickylee Thompson to a home visit to a single mum and her son who live in a one-bedroom rented flat not far from Wembley in order to understand the reality of her everyday life. Space and storage were the primary concerns and through these insights into how the majority of people really live, IKEA are able to offer 'Cool solutions people need'. And there was not a focus group in sight.

If arrogance leads to not wanting to listen, there is another different behaviour which in some ways can be equally damaging. Outsourcing listening to the customer to someone else. Too often a company thinks it is listening to its customers through conducting focus groups. I've been to a lot of focus groups in my career, although none for the last 10 years or so. Back in the day, what was called qualitative research was a useful balance to quantitative research. The latter was numbers based and remote. The former was real people reacting to something new. Be it a product or a new campaign. Indeed my earliest memory of a focus group is when I was still at school and my best mate became a recruiter. We would all go off in the same car to the house or venue and then arrive at 30-second intervals pretending not to know one another. I vividly recall being 'recruited' to test a new drink at the time which turned out to be Pernod and remember being suitably horrified when it turned colour after water was added. Years later, as the 'account man' I would have to sit in the room or behind a glass mirror, watching with bated breath as eight carefully selected people, representing the designated target audience, were shown the 'storyboard' of a new advertising campaign and waiting for their reactions. Like Roman emperors, was it going to be thumbs up or down? It was even worse if I had 'the client' sitting next to me. Thumbs up and it was all sweetness and light. Thumbs down and it was 'Spanish inquisition time' as panic set in on what to do next–and that was before I had to tell the bad news to the creatives that their beautiful baby had met its death in Feltham, Wolverhampton or Leeds, or wherever I had been the night before. That is not to say I haven't worked with some brilliant researchers whose skill lay in interpreting what was being said rather just reporting the bare facts. Equally true is that every so often insights were gleaned which made people think. I remember one such occasion when I was behind the mirror listening to a group of women who had been recruited from the less affluent parts of Kilburn, London. We were investigating the potential of a 'value' clothing store based on much lower prices but still with a fair degree of fashion and quality. The wine flowed readily and quite soon opinions started to emerge from everything to do with the state of their various marriages through to the education their kids were getting at the local schools. They were very quick witted and I was crying with laughter at some points. When it came to shopping one woman piped up with 'just because I don't have a lot of money, it doesn't mean I don't want to have a good experience and be treated properly and with respect when I buy something' (in reality there were a lot more f∗∗∗s involved, but you see the point). How true, I thought.

Over the years, the role of the focus group started to change. No longer a useful way to get some opinions, they started to become the voice of the 'customer' and in some cases became the only 'customer' a company would talk to. Brand managers at big FMCG firms were often guilty of this. Becoming quite lazy, sitting in the office and never talking directly with a customer but claiming they understood them and knew what they wanted. Steve Jobs was pretty scathing about the cult of the focus group, saying, 'You can't just ask customers what they want and then try to give that to them. By the time you get it built, they'll want something new',[15] and, to dramatise his way of thinking, 'We do no market research. We don't hire consultants. We just want to make great products'.[16] Of course, he did do market research but this was based on getting out to meet actual customers, understanding how they live and experiencing what's out there in order to get inspired with ideas. A bit like IKEA.

Amancio Ortega, the founder of Zara and Inditex fashion group, has the same philosophy. As quoted in *The Man From Zara*[17] about a trip to Israel, 'He wanted to stroll about the streets, see what women were wearing there, how they lived. We spent three days just soaking up the atmosphere. He wanted to be right, and he made every effort to be sure he was'. Knowing your customer is ingrained in the Zara and Inditex culture. The design team are constantly out:not in and aware and experiencing trends. They regularly visit university campuses, night clubs and other venues to see for themselves what's going on. When back at headquarters in Artexio, flatscreen televisions linked by webcam to offices in Shanghai, Tokyo and New York are constantly monitored looking out for trends. The 'Trends Team' never go to fashion shows but spend time tracking bloggers, whilst those in-store are trained and empowered to be at the forefront of their customer research. They listen intently and note down customer comments, ideas for cuts, fabric or a new line, and keenly observe new styles that its customers are wearing and have the potential to be converted into Zara styles. These insights then in turn get fed back to the design team, allowing products to be designed and developed to be of the moment.

Apple, IKEA and Zara. All massive global companies which have proved themselves to be sustainably successful partly because of the mindset of their respective founders. Get out there, listen and observe what is going on and become inspired by what is seen and heard, then come back and create the most wonderful products.

Being Brave yet Disciplined

One of my boyhood heroes was the Formula 1 driver Jim Clark. He won the world championship twice in the mid-1960s. He was suave to Graham Hill's somewhat rakish image. Jackie Stewart came along a few years later describing what made Clark such a good driver: 'He was so smooth, he was clean, he drove with such finesse. He never bullied a racing car, he sort of caressed it into doing the things he wanted to do'.[18] Not unlike fellow Scotsman Sean Connery's approach to playing James Bond.

I was reminded of this watching Sir Jackie Stewart talking on the BBC's 'The Andrew Marr Show' about the launch of the Race Against Dementia[19] scheme in partnership with Alzheimer's Research UK aimed at using the knowledge and know-how of the high-tech racing industry to help academics process data, promote rapid innovation and use artificial intelligence to boost research. When talking about this scheme he said,

We are striving to find answers that will avoid the heartache that we are experiencing, for millions in the future. In my career in motorsports, the innovations that I made possible, drove a safety revolution where many thought nothing could be done. I didn't accept the barriers to change then, and I don't accept them now. There are no problems, there are only solutions. The diseases behind dementia are complex and the challenge is high, but our ambition and ingenuity are higher, and the race against dementia is one we intend to win.[20]

It is this type of thinking that sits behind the third 'Best in Class' behaviour, 'Brave Yet Disciplined'.

This one is probably the toughest of the six. Lots of companies think they behave in a brave way. Even more think they behave in a disciplined way. In truth most companies do not do either very well and even fewer still operate in a way that is brave and disciplined at the same time. Bravery for me is to have courage and confidence in your ideas but the discipline to make sure that the implementation reflects the DNA of the company.

A quick way to land this point is by citing Apple Stores. The brave part was to go into retail in the first place. Frustrated at how their products were being presented, Apple essentially decided they could do it better. The discipline was they did it in an 'Apple' way and revolutionised the in-store experience in the same way that the iPod changed the way people thought about downloading and listening to music. The same DNA of design, simplicity and sheer attention to detail that goes into Apple products went into the Apple Store. My favourite anecdote is the use of stone flooring rather than wood. Remembering a visit to Florence, Italy, Steve Jobs wanted to replicate the experience in the stores. Not with any old stone but originated from the same quarry outside of Florence which supplied the city with its paving stones. This was partly for aesthetic reasons and partly as a statement of intent. Just like the pavements in Florence, Apple and Apple Stores would stand the test of time.

I am not sure if Steve Jobs ever met with Ron Dennis, who was the driving force behind the McLaren F1 team and founded McLaren Technology Group, but he certainly shared similar convictions and beliefs. I was hired to help the Leadership Team at McLaren Automotive create their own Company Spirit and although I never met with him, his 'spirit' was all-pervasive. My involvement was early on in the life of McLaren Automotive and was before the first car, the MP4-12C, had been launched. The company was at the start of a significant growth spurt which included a rapidly expanding workforce, and there was a recognition that to fulfil the long-term goals of creating an iconic car company, and to go into battle with, in particular, Ferrari, not just on the track but with road cars as well, it was important to build a strong culture. One rooted in McLaren F1 but one which gave McLaren Automotive its own sense of identity.

Nothing quite prepares you for your first visit to McLaren Technology Centre just outside Woking. It was designed by Lord Norman Foster, and I readily admit to going weak at the knees on arrival. Partly in awe and partly due to nerves not made any easier by the walk to reception. I have been to hundreds of receptions during the course of my career and nothing comes close to this experience. Once through the reception committee at security and having parked my Fiat 500, the walk takes you underground to be faced with a long white tunnel only interrupted halfway along by some fire doors. At the end of the tunnel there is a lift. Not any old lift but one that echoes the design of a piston. Still underground, the offices are two floors up, and as I ascended into the light I caught my first glimpse of the Boulevard which houses over 50 years of McLaren cars and the artificial lake, which I was to learn later is used to help cool the building. The walk from the lift to the reception area was on a suspended walkway. It was the stuff of dreams but also an embodiment of the company's design and engineering expertise. A far cry from the concrete bunker reception at Tesco.

This was Brave yet Disciplined in action. The bravery to build an F1 Team, to build the MTC, to create a car company but to do it with the disciplined attention to detail to make it feel McLaren. The building personified what I was later to understand as an obsession with breaking with convention and a culture of intelligent risk-taking. Courageous innovation rather than innovation for innovation's sake. When I started my work I talked to a number of employees. Some had been there from the start and others were quite new, and those in the latter group didn't really understand what lay behind some of the 'rules' at work. Personified by the clean desk policy whereby at the end of every day all paperwork needed to be out of sight, plus no food or drink was to be taken back to the desk. People put this down to 'Ron's obsessions' yet once I and the newer employees understood the reasoning behind this, both these requests made sense and reflected the culture and what became the McLaren Automotive Company Spirit. In essence, Ron Dennis wanted the building to look as good then as it was on the day it opened. After all, a potential sponsor might be walking through, and first impressions count. Clean desks at the end of the day helped to imbue a common ownership for how the place looked. Not just in the public spaces but back in the offices as well. The 'no coffee cups' rule also made sense. Each area had a beautifully designed coffee zone to encourage people to stand up, take a short break, enjoy their coffee and talk to people as they would if they were having an espresso in Rome or Milan. Not just take the coffee back to the desk, carry on working and not talk to anyone on the way as is the norm in most UK offices.

During the time I was involved, the McLaren Production Centre was being built. This became the factory for making the cars, and had the same sense of brave yet disciplined. The attention to detail was legendary and the absolute epitome of form and function working in perfect harmony. Beneath the production line floor there is the basement level for storage, and legend has it that when the floor was laid it was not absolutely perfect and had to be redone. Never mind that this floor would be covered by storage equipment and no longer visible. It was a principle at stake. Saying 'that will do' to the finish of the imperfect floor that will never be seen sets a precedence for poor behaviour, which in turn could lead to a breakdown of discipline in another part of the production of the car, which could ultimately impact on the customer experience. Caring about the smallest of details really did matter at McLaren.

So why is this the toughest of the six? Is it just about visionary leadership? After all, Steve Jobs and Ron Dennis are a rare breed. No, it was their and their teams' ability to behave as brave yet disciplined at the same time. They had an absolute clarity in what their company stood for and what made it different. Every decision is made easier by having a clear framework to operate in and a clear sense of purpose as to why. Not being clear about what the company stands for can lead to brave ideas which turn out to be foolhardy, and discipline which manifests itself as control.

Sir Jackie Stewart is not trying to build a company through the launch of 'The Race Against Dementia'; he is trying to help his wife, Helen, who has frontotemporal dementia, and others because he has discovered to his dismay not only is there no cure for dementia but it has been 16 years since the last dementia drug was developed. His brave idea is that he believes a cure for dementia will be found, and he has a clear sense of purpose of why he needs it. His discipline is to fall back on what he stood for when he was a three-time world champion racing driver.

In my career on the track, I saw staggering technological progress. Innovation was implemented at phenomenal pace. And whilst lap times were shaved, we also drove dramatic developments in safety that saved lives. At times, the resistance to change was incredible, but we simply had to rise to the challenge of halting the record of deaths. When problems arose, we didn't accept defeat, and answers were found. This gave me a trust in determination, and a belief that it can, and will, be brought to bear in dementia research. I'm committed to making this possible.[21]

Amen to that.

Notes

1. 'How United Turned the Friendly Skies into a Flying Hellscape', *Wired*, 13 April 2017, https://www.wired.com/2017/04/uniteds-greed-turned-friendly-skies-flying-hellscape/

2. Carroll, Dave. 'United Breaks Guitars', YouTube, 6 July 2009, https://www.youtube.com/watch?v=5YGc4zOqozo

3. 'Big Banks Roll Out 14 Promises in "Customer Charter"', The Financial Brand, 23 June 2010, https://thefinancialbrand.com/12348/rbs-natwest-14-point-customer-charter/

4. 'What does the TSB fiasco tell us about banking in Britain?', *The Guardian*, 27 April 2018, https://www.theguardian.com/business/2018/apr/27/tsb-it-meltdown-banking

5. Gerrards Cross Tunnel, Wikipedia, https://en.wikipedia.org/wiki/Gerrards_Cross_Tunnel

6. 'Former Tesco managers go on trial accused of overstating profits', *The Guardian*, 8 October 2008, https://www.theguardian.com/business/2018/oct/08/former-tesco-managers-go-on-trial-accused-of-overstating-profits

7. Shah, Oliver. 'A toxic culture was the real villain at Tesco', *The Times,* 27 January 2019, https://www.thetimes.co.uk/article/oliver-shah-a-toxic-culture-was-the-real-villain-at-tesco-xqslr22mg

8. Hsieh, Tony. 'Delivering Happiness: A Path to Profits, Passion and Purpose', Business Plus, 6 July 2010.

9. 'Jeff Bezos quotes', Goodreads, https://www.goodreads.com/quotes/7383200-your-brand-is-what-other-people-say-about-you-when

10. 'HMV deaf to internet threat', *The Sunday Times,* 20 January 2013, https://www.thetimes.co.uk/article/hmv-deaf-to-internet-threat-jdt9vlpgwpt

11. 'Sir Richard Greenbury obituary', *The Guardian*, 28 September 2017, https://www.theguardian.com/business/2017/sep/28/sir-richard-greenbury-obituary

12. Bevan, Judy. 'The Rise and Fall of Marks and Spencer', Profile Books, May 2002.

13. 'IKEA Facts and Figures 2018', https://www.ikea.com/gb/en/this-is-ikea/about-us/ikea-facts-and-figures-2018-pubfd3597c1

14. 'IKEA Our vision and business idea', https://www.ikea.com/ms/en_JP/about_ikea/the_ikea_way/our_business_idea/index.html

15. 'Steve Jobs quotes', BrainyQuote, https://www.brainyquote.com/quotes/steve_jobs_161994

16. 'Steve Jobs quotes', Wonderful quote, https://www.wonderfulquote.com/a/steve-jobs-quotes

17. O'Shea, Covadonga *The Man from Zara: The Story of the Genius Behind the Inditex Group*, Lid Publishing, March 2012.

18. 'The Importance of being Jim Clark', *Influx*, https://www.influx.co.uk/features/the-importance-of-being-jim-clark/

19. 'Sir Jackie Stewart opens up on his wife Lady Helen's dementia', 'The Andrew Marr Show', BBC, 14 October 2018, https://www.bbc.co.uk/programmes/p06nv3fq

20. 'Formula One teams race to help beat Alzheimer's', *The Telegraph*, 14 October 2018, https://www.telegraph.co.uk/news/2018/10/13/formula-one-teams-race-help-beat-alzheimers/

21. 'Formula One teams race to help beat Alzheimer's', *The Telegraph*, 14 October 2018, https://www.telegraph.co.uk/news/2018/10/13/formula-one-teams-race-help-beat-alzheimers/

8

Love Is Still in the Air

Three down and three to go. Each one of the behaviours we have looked at helps companies become relevant for the needs and wants of employees and customers today, so let us explore the second half.

Innovating. Constantly

Once upon a time in UK retailing, there was the doctrine of the 'cookie cutter'. In essence, this meant 'let's work on optimising the look, feel and the product range in our store and then roll the same out everywhere'. Although this had the virtue of creating consistency in the experience a customer had, it also froze that experience in time. The store stood still whilst everything around it moved on. A quote from John F. Kennedy comes to mind: 'For time and the world do not stand still. Change is the law of life. And those who look only to the past or the present are certain to miss the future'.[1]

Technology has changed both the world we live in and the context we operate in. Given the sheer pace of technological change over the last 50 years, standing still is no longer a viable strategy. Not when so much has happened so quickly. Just in case we need reminding. Google Driverless cars (now called Waymo) are on trial in Phoenix, Arizona. In the summer of 2016, Amazon started trials of delivering with drones. NASA created the first prototype of a large-format affordable 3D printer in 2013. The iPhone was launched in June 2007. Twitter in March 2006. In November 2006 Tesla was unveiled at the San Francisco Auto Show. Facebook started in August 2004. Google in 1998. Amazon in 1994. August 1991 saw British computer scientist Tim

© The Author(s) 2020
M. Cox, *The Business Case for Love*, https://doi.org/10.1007/978-3-030-36426-7_8

Berners-Lee post a short summary of the World Wide Web project on the alt. hypertext newsgroup, inviting collaborators. Apollo 11 landed on the Moon on 20 July 1969, with Neil Armstrong uttering famously, 'One small step for man, one giant leap for mankind'.[2] Seven years earlier, JFK announced to a crowd at Rice University Football stadium,

> We choose to go to the moon! We choose to go to the moon in this decade and do the other things, not because they are easy, but because they are hard; because that goal will serve to organize and measure the best of our energies and skills, because the challenge is one that we are willing to accept, one we are unwilling to postpone, and one we intend to win, and the others, too.[3]

Anybody old enough will remember where they were when the moon landing happened. I was at school, and together with all pupils and teachers was ushered into the Assembly Hall to watch. Millions, perhaps billions, also watched wherever people could find a TV set.

A moment recreated in the excellent 2018 film *First Man*, which tells the story of the sacrifices and the cost of fulfilling JFK's vision. What stood out when watching the film was the sheer bravery of those involved and the technological advancement since those days. The rockets seemed to be held together by rivets and sticky-backed plastic. It was all switches and levers. An analogue and binary system which makes the achievement even more remarkable.

The 50th anniversary of the moon landing reinforces how much innovation has happened since Neil Armstrong spoke to the world. The results of innovation are all around us, yet it terrifies most businesses. They struggle with what it means, let alone how to do it. Preferring the comfort of the status quo. The known not the unknown. The tangible and the measurable. They think it is a process to 'buy in' or 'outsource'. They are scared of failure so prefer to sit on their hands. They know how to say 'no' but struggle with 'no, but have you thought of this'. They want it to be rational, logical and in a straight line, whereas to be innovative the reality needed is a creative and organic way of behaving. Most of all this terror comes from thinking innovation is only about creating something completely new, be it a product or service. They look at Apple and just say we can't do that.

The truth is that most innovation comes from thinking in a different way. Less 'a leap for mankind', more a quest for continuous improvement. Or put another way, keeping the customer experience fresh. Google is my 'go-to' company to land this point. They exemplify the Best in Class behaviour of 'Innovate. Constantly', and the mindset that goes with it. Google spends a lot on Research and Development. Under the guise of its recently adopted company name Alphabet, it spent \$16.62 billion, equivalent to 15% of its revenue during 2017.[4] Part of this is spent on the next big breakthrough. Driverless cars and Artificial Intelligence. But Google do what a lot of companies fail to do in that they look after and constantly invest in their 'core' product. The one that made them famous. The one that most people will know them by. In their case, it is 'search'. Google has captured 88%[5] of the global market for search, handling more than three billion searches a day according to their own statistics. Google know that no matter how many successful products they launch, most people will access the company via some form of search. It is most customers' way into the company and often the first building block in creating trust and for some 'love'. That is why they invest so heavily in keeping their core product fresh. The search engine experience has changed imperceptibly over time but has been continuously improved. Only by looking back on the 'search experience' of 10 years ago and comparing it with today do you realise how big the difference is. This is their stated 70/20/10 model,[6] which has been in existence since the early days, in action. Seventy percent of projects are dedicated to the core business. Twenty percent of projects relate to the core business. Ten percent of projects are unrelated to the core business.

Another way Google keeps the customer experience for search fresh happened originally more by accident than design. The Google Doodle. The first one honoured the Burning Man festival in 1998 and was designed by founders Larry Page and Sergey Brin to notify users of their absence in case the servers crashed. Over the next few years the Google Doodle became an institution and is used to celebrate artists, scientists, well-known events and holidays. It kept the often daily experience of visiting the home page fresh, and what was fun on the surface was always connected back into search. Scrolling the cursor onto the Doodle allows you to find out more about the event or person. This approach also broke all traditional rules associated with branding, namely that the logo was sacrosanct. A point Douglas Edwards muses about in his entertaining book *I'm Feeling Lucky: The Confessions of Google Employee Number 59*.[7]

> Our users loved the randomness of the logo artwork and sent us dozens of appreciative emails. Google's brilliant strategy of humanizing an otherwise sterile interface with cute little cartoon features was an enormous hit—and as the company's online brand manager, the person responsible for building Google's awareness and brand equity, I had opposed it as adamantly as I could. Yes, if it had been left to me, there would be no Google Doodles at all; just our cold stiff logo lying in state, wrapped in a sheet of pristine white pixels. It was so blindingly obvious (to me) that I was right, yet I was so clearly wrong. Google did

that to you – made you challenge all your assumptions and experience-based beliefs until you began to wonder if up was really up, or if it might not actually be a different kind of down.

The Google Doodle and the Google Driverless Car are both forms of innovation, just from different ends of the spectrum. Both are needed but Google know that looking after the core matters most of all. Without investing in the former, the latter is less likely to succeed.

Ultimately innovation is about having an idea and bringing that to life. Having an idea in the first place normally comes from gaining an insight. The 'light bulb moment' that comes from listening to people or observing what is happening around you. A point dramatised rather neatly in the film *The Social Network* when the actor playing Mark Zuckerberg is asked by a fellow student if he knows whether a certain other student is going out with anyone. Which of course inspires him to add 'relationship status' to the Facebook page and the rest, as they say, is history.

Simply put, the more a company has a culture of listening, the more insights it will have and the more ideas it will be able to create. Think of it this way and it is not so terrifying after all. Yet as we saw in the previous chapter, when there is something wrong with the company culture, listening almost always stops. Without insights there are no new ideas so the customer experience stagnates and the company will eventually, or perhaps all of a sudden, wither and die.

Back at Google, listening, having insights and getting feedback are building blocks to their innovative culture. They see innovation as an iterative process. Have an idea, test it, get feedback and evolve the original idea to take into account the feedback. Google took inspiration for this, not from other technology companies, but from the restaurant business and what they call a 'soft opening'. Instead of hoping everything will be all right on the big first night, a new restaurant will have a few days or weeks where they invite people in, learn what works, discover what customers love and build from there into what they hope will be a place people will come back to, time and again.

As with restaurants that need to regularly change their menus, the music business is another example of a category that cannot afford to stand still. Every week brings new releases, new bands, new music. Some are one-hit wonders whilst others stand the test of time, and it is to a true rock star that I turn as my last example of how to innovate constantly. Sadly, I never saw David Bowie perform. My wife did, in her younger days. I was a fan. She adored him. The world was a sadder place on 10 January 2016 as news of his death ricocheted around the globe. A career spanning four decades and considered to be one of the most influential musicians of the twentieth century, acclaimed by critics and fellow musicians, particularly for his innovative work during the 1970s. His career was marked by reinvention and visual presentation and record sales estimated at 140 million records, making him one of the world's best-selling artists.

The closest I got to him was when we both attended the V&A Exhibition 'David Bowie Is' a year or so before his death. Brilliantly curated, it told his story through artefacts, props, costumes and, of course, his music. It became the museum's fastest-selling show and as of 2018 holds the record for being the most visited exhibit in the V&A Museum's history.[8] The exhibition went on tour and over its five-year run, it stopped at 12 museums around the world and attracted over 2 million visitors. What made it so special was that David Bowie's approach to life was his sheer determination to succeed. Success did not come easily for him. There were several false starts, but he did not give up. Indeed, he seemed to gain strength from each experience, taking with him the insights he had learned and enjoyed to shape his next attempt at 'making it'. He must have had massive inner drive and confidence in his own ability. He knew success would come from being different. Standing out from the crowd rather than fading into it. Failure was not an option, even when success was a long way around the corner.

When success did come, he never stood still and completely rejected the notion of the 'cookie cutter'. He was always out:not in. Being inquisitive. Embracing new experiences. Listening to, hearing and seeing what was around him. Taking on new challenges. Harnessing technology to keep his message modern and relevant to new generations. Rarely stuck. Leading not following. Never copying. He would avoid the obvious and look for the unexpected. Always changing. Always innovating.

So for those struggling with the concept of innovation, perhaps it is time to channel your own inner Ziggy Stardust, become a hero and hopefully for more than just one day!

Creating Memorable Customer Experiences

Steve Jobs understood the fundamental importance and role of the customer experience. 'You've got to start with the customer experience and work backwards to the technology. You can't start with the technology and try to figure out where you're going to sell it'[9] is perhaps the quote of his I use the most in my work. Lesser known but equally important in a different way is the one accredited to Rand Fishkin, CEO and Founder of Moz and SparkToro: 'Best way to sell something – don't sell anything. Earn the awareness, respect and trust of those who might buy'.[10] These two quotes from someone very well known and someone less so are offering simple, straightforward advice, yet most companies do the opposite. They are stuck in the mindset of 'Here is our product, how are we going to sell it?' Why do they do this, when all the evidence points to those companies who start with the customer experience and work backwards doing rather well? Apple is after all the first trillion dollar company. In my experience those in the 'How are we going to sell it?' camp are there because there is little ambition beyond trying to make a profit and survive, and certainly no broader sense of purpose around what the company is trying to achieve.

Whole Foods Market is more in the Steve Jobs mould. Their sense of purpose is an extension of its motto 'Whole Foods, Whole People, Whole Planet'. To me this is clear, simple and directional. Perhaps not surprising given the founder, John Mackey, believes in the notion of 'Conscious Capitalism'[11] and that 'Great Companies have great purposes'. He is also clear about the connection between the vision and profit. 'Just as people cannot live without eating, so a business cannot live without profits. But most people don't live to eat, and neither must businesses live just to make profits'.[12]

I must admit that it is only recently that I have become a fan of Whole Foods. It first launched in London back in 2007 at Kensington High Street, which is just a stone's throw from where Prince William and Kate live. When I first went to the store I found it quite controlling. A bit holier than thou. All a bit knitted muesli. My reappraisal of Whole Foods started when I included it as part of my 'Memorable Customer Experience Events' and the almost always positive comments I received from my clients who went there. What accelerated this was our experience in Australia when visiting our daughter, Sophie, when she was living and studying in Sydney.

I first went to Australia around 15 years ago on business to visit a client in Melbourne. I went for only five days, which, given the 24-hour flying time there and back, was nothing short of ridiculous. I enjoyed it but I distinctly remember feeling that the country in general, and particularly the customer experience, was lagging behind the UK. Having made the journey again twice over the last couple of years, my sense is that the roles have been reversed. Australia comes across as a country with its best years ahead and the emphasis on customer experience is, more often than not, leading not following. Particularly when it comes to food and what seems to have become a national obsession with coffee, which frankly puts the UK to shame. There are no ubiquitous chains other than Starbucks, which survives only through tourists. People choose their coffee store based on the blend and the choice of the coffee bean. All baristas know how to make coffee. All know how to smile and make some small talk. Particularly if they want a bit of 'pom bashing' with some well-timed comments about the cricket. Proving that a memorable customer experience does not have to be a big thing. A smile and a great cup of coffee go a long way.

Shopping for food is also quite different. A visit to Harris Farms is a must. A family-run business in New South Wales selling fruit and vegetables with a butcher and fishmonger as part of the offer. If that sounds like an old-fashioned grocery store then you would be right, but this one is wrapped up in their belief in nature itself. The land, the sea, the air, the elements are very much part of a Sydneysider lifestyle, and they reflect this within their focus on what is in season and what is locally sourced. In many ways, in the parts of Australia we visited, the 'Whole Foods' concept has gone mainstream. It was not difficult to find shops with aisle upon aisle of healthy and nutritious food. Gluten free is everywhere (not just stuck 'on the naughty step' as in the UK), as is vegan. All things 'coconut' seem to be on every aisle end. As is gut-friendly kombucha. Healthy eating is the new 'ready meal'. Acai, goji berries and other 'super foods' are the new normal. All this can be easily found in an average Woolworths store two hours out from Sydney. Yes of course there are frozen pizzas, tinned vegetables and sugary drinks. But the balance is significantly different. Yes they have price promotions but the customer experience is not dominated by price alone as is the case with UK food retailing. There is a feeling of choice, ideas, value and service. In a smiley not a surly way.

Revisiting Whole Foods when back in the UK, I can now see their vision in action. They want to help their customers have a healthy lifestyle. They want food to be produced in a sustainable way that is good for the planet. They've stopped being snooty and come across as welcoming. They want you to eat healthily but to have a good time as well. When did you last feel that at any other mainstream UK supermarket? Back to John Mackey: 'For us, our most important stakeholder is not our stockholders, it is our customers. We're in business to serve the needs and desires of our core customer base'.[13] So the moral of the story is that by focussing on creating memorable customer experiences, good things happen. Not just from a customer perspective but from a financial one too. Amazon came calling in 2017 and spent $13.7 billion on acquiring the company.[14] Not bad for a business which started with one store in Austin, Texas, in 1980.

Another example of a company which prides itself on their customer experience is Singapore Airlines. It had always been on my personal bucket list to fly with them, influenced partly by the advertising extolling the virtues of 'Singapore Girl. You're A Great Way To Fly', and this particular item was ticked off the list on our last trip to Sydney. As I told my wife, choosing to fly with them would be a good way to check out whether the 'image and experience' matched, although Karen did not take much convincing. Our trip did not start well as on the morning of our departure it started to snow. By the time we got to Heathrow it was starting to settle and as everyone in the UK knows, put the words 'snow' and 'Heathrow' together and it will end in tears. Once again, having been surprised by the concept of winter and that every so often it snows, chaos reigned. Luckily that did not include our flight as we took off only an hour or so late, but on landing in Singapore the next morning we found out that whoever had opted to fly British Airways had largely gone nowhere. One hundred and seventy flights cancelled, affecting 50,000 people mainly because British Airways could not get their planes de-iced.[15] Meanwhile, back in the air and on our way to Singapore the image and the experience were in perfect harmony, helped along by a Singapore Sling. Interestingly, and this was the case for all four flights, we flew on an original A380, which meant the product (the plane, the seats, the in-flight amenities) was starting to show its age. A like-for-like comparison with Etihad, with whom we had flown on our previous trip down under, would be unfavourable. However, their point of difference was the in-flight team. It was the people who made the customer experience memorable. Singapore Airlines, just like Apple and Whole Foods, start with their vision for the customer experience and work backwards. Accordingly, Singapore Airlines had in place for years the concept of 'customer first', which is all about tailoring the service, customising it and personalising it to make sure it's a meaningful experience for the customer. This became the cornerstone for one of their brand campaigns.[16]

And that's exactly what happened. My abiding memory of not just this leg to Singapore but onwards to Sydney and back again a few weeks later was the sense that each member of the crew was 'in the moment', reacting to what was happening at that exact moment in a human and helpful, not subservient, way. The exact opposite to how I feel about most other airline experiences. It comes as no surprise that Singapore Airlines has been named 'World's Best Airline' in the 2018 Skytrax Awards,[17] although in the 2019 equivalent they have been pipped to top spot by Qatar. This is the fourth time they have been awarded the No 1 spot and it coincided with the company achieving their highest profits in seven years with a 148% increase,[18] which shows that by focussing on what makes the company different rather than competing as a commodity experience based just on price, everyone wins. The customers, the employees and the shareholders.

Looking back, the ability for the Singapore Airlines team to be 'in the moment' and adapt to the situation in front of them was all the more admirable after Karen and I had spent four days in Singapore during our stopover.

Hosted by Martin Mackay and his irrepressible wife, Yelena, this was our first time in Singapore. Martin has been my client three times and he was based there at the time. We have become firm friends, and rather amusingly, as a result of working together, he is now absolutely wedded to the concept of a memorable customer experience. Constantly commenting on the good, the bad and the downright ugly. What became apparent during our stay was that although on the surface standards of customer service in Singapore are extremely high, most Singaporeans are not great at being 'in the moment'. Everything is fine if both the customer and the employee stick to the script but if something untoward happens the mask slips and panic can set in. The one really touristy thing we did was the four of us had Chili Crab. It was during this experience that we went a little off-piste and ordered wine and not the expected beer. This seemed to cause consternation in the ranks. First it was pointed out to our host that most of the wine on the wine list did not exist and then when we had found a bottle available it took an age to arrive. Then there was trouble both in finding a corkscrew and then a waiter capable of using it as this seemed to be beyond the ability of the 'wine waiter'. Much to the merriment of the four of us. Martin then regaled us with other similar stories, which means the training at Singapore Airlines must be quite remarkable as they are not only seemingly overcoming a cultural norm but they actually use the notion of 'being in the moment' as a real point of difference.

Creating a memorable customer experience can come in many forms, and I suspect a number of shareholders and company bosses would struggle with the notion of the 'Best way to sell something: don't sell anything' quote at the beginning of this section. Yet that is precisely the approach taken by another personal favourite, the Australian skincare company Aesop. Originally from Melbourne, there are now over 180 stores worldwide and I've been to a fair few. From Covent Garden, London, to Newtown, Sydney, to Flinders Lane, Melbourne, and Jakobsbergsgatan, Stockholm, amongst others. Part of their success is their philosophy of 'unselling'. They refuse to deliver false promises, like eternal beauty, and focus instead on that old-fashioned proposition of a quality product and knowledgeable staff. They promote themselves through storytelling, paying homage to the inspiration for their name, Aesop and his Fables. They rarely, if ever, discount. They use design as part of their difference, with each store unique and reflecting the community it sits within. Using established architects and local vernacular to achieve this to create a feeling and an experience through layout, material use and interesting refreshments which are offered up during a visit. Its largest store is in the Broadway Theatre District in downtown Los Angeles, where the walls are lined with reclaimed cardboard tubing from fabric rolls discarded by the nearby fashion district and other elements of the store's interior are made entirely from recycled paper. Minimising their environmental impact is very much part of the Aesop ethos. 'We try to stay true to the indigenous (Aboriginal) saying "touch the ground lightly"', says Founder Dennis Paphitis.[19] This links back to their business success and Paphitis' belief that 'there is a direct correlation between interesting, captivating store spaces and customer traffic within a store'.

I know from personal experience that, no matter where you are in the world, Aesop make their customers feel special and welcomed, and their staff really do know all about their products and what to recommend in an 'unselling' way. As an example, I recall going into the Covent Garden store in London and asking this hipster chap with a wonderful beard about their shaving serum. He was rhapsodic about it from his own experience of using it and I was thinking to myself 'but he has a beard' when I realised that he wasn't talking about shaving his face!

Perhaps the most remarkable aspect about Aesop is that it is a private equity success story, so they can happen. In 2010 Harbert Australia Private Equity brought a minority stake in the company. In December 2012, Aesop sold a 65% stake to Brazilian company Natura for $71.6 million. Natura took total ownership in December 2016.[20] So the moral of this particular story is that by understanding and adopting the mindset of 'don't sell anything', lots of sales happen!

Ensuring Personal and Company Values Match

There is a scene towards the end of the 2013 film *The Internship* which neatly brings to life this last, but by no means least, 'Best in Class' company behaviour. It's a film about two recently laid-off car salesmen who attempt to get a job at Google. It's not a great film, although it has some funny moments and it does have a clear message. Namely, it's not just about being smart or the brightest but whether the person hoping to get employed fits the Google culture. Do they have Googleness?

The point is demonstrated through the decision not to hire the know-it-all 'college jock' for the internship, who despite coming out with top marks, is deemed not to have the required amount of Googleness. Leaving our two heroes to claim the prize of the opportunity to work for Google because their attitude fits the culture of the company.

The film illustrates the point that companies with a strong culture know that this is a precious commodity. They work hard to nurture it and look after it as they grow. They recruit not just for someone's skills or attributes, but for fit. Do they fit our culture? Failure to do this means that the culture starts to get watered down and what was once a strength becomes a weakness. Company culture is much more than getting on with your fellow employees. It's a framework for decision making which should allow people to understand whether what they are doing is right. If it fits the culture, the Company Spirit, then do it. If not, don't.

I firmly believe this works both ways. We all have our own Personal Spirit. Our own set of values, sense of purpose and beliefs. Some of us are very cognisant of this. For others it may be more buried. Most people when they look back at their careers will highlight times when it just sort of clicked, and normally this was when their personal values and the values of the company they worked for were aligned. This was brought home to me during my work with McLaren Automotive. Around about the same time as my involvement some engineers had been hired from BMW. These people were highly skilled but pretty soon it became obvious that it was not going to work out. This was nothing to do with the quality of their work or that they were bad people, rather that they didn't fit the McLaren Automotive culture. Which, in my opinion, although serene on the surface, was a hugely energised, very creative and dynamic place to work. The ex-BMW people were more 'straight-edge' and, well, 'Germanic', and hence struggled with their working environment, and they subsequently left. This experience meant that McLaren Automotive started to pay a lot more attention to looking for the right fit as well as the required skills when recruiting new people.

Perhaps the best known example in the UK is the John Lewis Partnership both within the John Lewis department stores and its sister supermarket company Waitrose. It offers a partnership approach for their employees with people having a stake in the success of the business. They also have a strong set of values and behaviours which they use to recruit the right people. Although both parts of the business seem to have had their wobbles recently, this approach seems to largely work. One of my clients had worked at John Lewis and he gave me an interesting insight. He said most people ended up working for the company either for a few months or for their whole career. In other words some get through the interview process but quite quickly work out that it is not for them. Whilst others arrive and think wow, I love this, and stay for a long time.

Not far from the John Lewis store in Oxford Street, London, sits Niketown on the corner of Oxford Circus. It's been a flagship store for Nike ever since it first opened back in 1999. It was also one of the first companies to recruit for fit not just skills. A friend of mine at the time was the manager at the Marks & Spencer across the road from Niketown, and being a sociable chap he did what most store managers would do and went to say hello to his opposite number at the about to be opened Niketown. During their conversation the subject of recruitment came up and this was at a time when the first question asked to any potential employee, particularly in retail, was 'Who else have you worked for?' My friend learnt that Nike's first question turned out to be 'Who won the Men's 100-meter final at the Atlanta Olympics three years earlier in 1996?' The story goes that if you didn't know the answer, you never got to question 2! Whether this is an apocryphal story or not, it made sense. Nike is a sports company, with its roots in athletics, and it wanted to recruit people who loved and knew a lot about sport to represent it at Niketown. So if you did not take a keen interest in athletics then you were not right for Nike. Apparently Nike still use a version of this today, with the first question being 'Who is your favourite Nike-endorsed athlete?' The answer, by the way, to the 1999 question is Canadian Donovan Bailey.

As I have said before, I have had the privilege of working with hundreds of people over the years and it is my belief that the vast majority of employees want to work for a company with a clear set of values, beliefs and sense of purpose. They want their company to have a strong culture and to feel part of it. Most are no longer prepared to work in a toxic environment, particularly millennials, who are most likely to vote with their feet and find a place more in keeping with their own values.

At the absolute epicentre of this 'Best in Class' behaviour are people, so it saddens me that recruitment companies and HR directors who one would think should be at the forefront of embracing what most employees now want are often stuck in the old ways of doing things. There are of course honourable exceptions but I have lost count of the number of people I know who moan about the current recruitment process. They think it is a very transactional experience and still a numbers game, with the recruiter focussed on filling the brief rather than truly understanding the needs, wants and values of the individual. Candidates who are often senior people and feel that the primary focus of the recruiter remains the 'head' side of the CV. All of the attention is on achievements and targets met in previous roles, with little if any time spent on the 'heart' side. Understanding their Personal Spirit so that they can be better placed with an emphasis on the cultural fit. Both sides are important of course but given that the companies that are succeeding today tend to 'lead with the heart and follow with the head', this is a backward-looking approach. It's equally true of HR directors. This is perhaps the role that has changed the most over the last 20 years. The most enlightened HR directors are the ones that fundamentally get the importance of the company culture and often position themselves to be joined at the hip with the CEO as the keepers of the company flame. The majority do not, either through lack of ability or belief. They choose to focus on the more traditional aspects of the HR role: employee reviews and benefits.

Patrick Bermingham, HR Director at McLaren Technology Group, definitely sits in the former camp. It was he who recognised the need to create a sense of 'One Team' at McLaren Automotive, which led to the brief, and ultimately my appointment, to help with the 'kick-off' of this approach.

On the recruitment side, Steve Hyde, through his company 360xec, personifies the opposite of the transactional headhunter. Steve and I go back a long way and worked together on the development of the Personal Spirit approach. He absolutely operates with the balance of heart and head in understanding and placing his candidates so that Personal Values and Company Values match. He can't be right all of the time but boy does he try!

So there you have it. The six 'Best in Class' company behaviours, and those who embrace this mindset do not pick and choose. They try to live all of the six, all of the time. Let's recap on what this means.

Table 8.1 The six 'Best in Class' company behaviours

Ensuring image and experience match	Start by getting crystal clear on what makes the company different and what it stands for. Then make sure this is reflected throughout all communication and the actual customer experience. Say what you do, and do what you say.
Being constantly inside the heads of customers	Get out from the desk, cut down on the meetings. Be out. Not In. Be curious. Talk, listen and understand what people are thinking and how people live their lives.
Being brave yet disciplined	Have courage and bravery in your ideas. The confidence to do something new but have the discipline to make sure that what the company does fits with what the company stands for.
Innovating. Constantly.	The more people listen, the more insights they get and the more ideas they will have. Bring them to life. Look after the 'core'. This helps the company feel fresh and contemporary. Strive for what the company wants to be, not where it is happy to settle.
Creating memorable customer experiences	Start with the customer experience the company wants to create, and work backwards to the product offered. That way the customer and their experience remains at the very heart of every decision made.
Ensuring personal and company values match	Recruit for fit not just skills. Create a culture of curious employees that share the values of the company and want to be part of the story. The stronger the culture becomes the more people will start to self-select. If they do not fit they will tend to leave and look for a place more in keeping with their own personal values.

Live the mindset of all six 'Best in Class' company behaviours and love will be very much in the air! For employees, for customers and even for shareholders. Just ask anybody who has invested in Apple, Google, Amazon, Whole Foods Market, Singapore Airlines or Aesop.

Notes

1. 'John F. Kennedy quotes', BrainyQuote, https://www.brainyquote.com/quotes/john_f_kennedy_135392
2. 'Neil Armstrong quotes', BrainyQuote, https://www.brainyquote.com/quotes/neil_armstrong_101137
3. 'John F. Kennedy Moon Speech-Rice Stadium', 12 September 1962, https://er.jsc.nasa.gov/seh/ricetalk.htm
4. '6 Companies Spending the Most on R&D', Nasdaq, 8 August 2018, https://www.nasdaq.com/articles/6-companies-spending-most-rd-2018-08-08
5. 'Worldwide desktop market share of leading search engines from January 2010 to July 2019', Statista, https://www.statista.com/statistics/216573/worldwide-market-share-of-search-engines/
6. 'The 70:20:10 Innovation Rule', Now Go Create, 18 February 2015, https://www.nowgocreate.co.uk/the-702010-innovation-rule/
7. Edwards, Douglas. *I'm Feeling Lucky: The Confessions of Google Employee Number 59*, 2011, Allen Lane
8. 'David Bowie exhibition breaks V&A record', BBC News, 8 November 2016, https://www.bbc.co.uk/news/entertainment-arts-37907055
9. 'Steve Jobs quotes', Quotefancy, https://quotefancy.com/quote/911790/Steve-Jobs-You-ve-got-to-start-with-the-customer-experience-and-work-backwards-to-the
10. 'Rand Fishkin quotes', Pinterest, https://www.pinterest.co.uk/pin/110760472059346160/
11. 'Conscious Capitalism: Creating a New Paradigm for Business', Whole Foods Market, John Mackey, 9 November 2006, https://www.wholefoodsmarket.com/blog/john-mackeys-blog/conscious-capitalism-creating-new-paradigm-for%C2%A0business
12. 'How Whole Foods CEO John Mackey is Leading a Revolution in Health and Business', *Entrepreneur*, 3 January 2019, https://www.entrepreneur.com/article/325128
13. '11 Inspiring John Mackey Quotes for Small Business', Logomaker, 25 March 2013, https://www.logomaker.com/blog/2013/03/25/11-inspiring-quotes-for-small-business-from-john-mackey/

14. 'Amazon is buying Whole Foods for $13.7 Billion', Forbes, 16 June 2017, https://www.forbes.com/sites/laurengensler/2017/06/16/amazon-to-buy-whole-foods-for-13-7-billion/

15. 'BA cancels more than 100 Heathrow flights after snow and ice', *The Guardian,* 11 December 2017, https://www.theguardian.com/uk-news/2017/dec/11/british-airways-cancels-100-flights-snow-ice-delayed

16. 'Singapore Airlines Launches New Brand Campaign', Singapore Airlines, 2 September 2013, https://www.singaporeair.com/en_UK/gb/media-centre/press-release/article/?q=en_UK/2013/July-September/02Sep2013-1020

17. 'SIA Named "World's Best Airline" in 2018 Skytrax Awards' Singapore Airlines, https://www.singaporeair.com/en_UK/us/media-centre/press-release/article/?q=en_UK/2018/July-September/ne2318-180717

18. 'Singapore Airlines beats expectations with highest profit in seven years', Reuters, 17 May 2018, https://uk.reuters.com/article/us-singapore-air-results/singapore-airlines-beats-expectations-with-highest-profit-in-seven-years-idUKKCN1II19R

19. 'Film Director Luca Guadagnino collaborates with Aesop on new Rome store', *Wallpaper,* 28 September 2018, https://www.wallpaper.com/lifestyle/aesop-rome-store-opens

20. Aesop (brand), Wikipedia, https://en.wikipedia.org/wiki/Aesop_(brand)

9

The 'Love' Grid

Perhaps not surprisingly, I work hard at living the six 'Best in Class' company behaviours. Especially when working with my clients. When I founded The Company Spirit, I spent a lot of time talking and listening to current and potential clients. As with any business, I was both trying to sharpen the actual proposition around what made The Company Spirit different and creating a tone of voice and language which was my own, rather than borrowed. The more I talked and listened the clearer I became. As I found out, it was important not just to listen to other people, but also to myself. Whether in business or in life, we all say things that the other person or people we are talking with instantly 'get'. Equally, there are times when that does not happen.

The trick is to remember the phrases that click. Indeed the language I use when talking to a potential client for the first time and the language I am most known for by my clients has come about when I have said something, often spontaneously, that works! 'Kick off' is one such example. My approach is the opposite of traditional 'consulting' whereby the goal often seems to be to stay involved for as long as possible, and rather it is to create a significant impact early on and then give my clients a framework they can largely follow themselves.

I think the first time I used this phrase was when I was under consideration by the leadership team of Kraft Foods in Scandinavia. They were looking for some help in bringing alive the values which had largely been created in the USA, to become relevant for people living and working in Denmark, Finland, Norway and Sweden. Out of my mouth popped the phrase 'kick off' to my potential Kraft clients when I was on a phone call. It clearly helped to explain to them not just what I did but how I went about it, so I continued to use it.

© The Author(s) 2020
M. Cox, *The Business Case for Love*, https://doi.org/10.1007/978-3-030-36426-7_9

A few months later when I received the phone call to say I had won the 'pitch' to work with the McLaren Automotive Team, part of the feedback was that they liked the term 'kick off' as that was what they needed. They did not want a person or a company to be there for months or years to come, they just needed some help to get them going.

The word I use a lot which has always been the most polarising is 'love'. More than once I was asked to replace the word 'love' with something else in a written proposal for fear of what members of their leadership team might say. Men, in particular, have struggled with the idea of 'love' and 'business'. However, given 'love' is part of my core beliefs, I wasn't going to replace it. I just needed to find a way of explaining in simple terms what I meant by it so that it wasn't, in the immortal words of Louise Barnes, when she was CEO at Fat Face, then Crew Clothing Company and most recently as Investor Director at Beaufort & Blake, seen as 'Fluffy HR Bollocks'. Part of my solution was to create the phrase 'The Business Case for Love' as my headline for the philosophy and approach I have developed and believe in. A deliberate juxtaposition, which sets out to explain that the result of this way of working is a long-term, sustainable, commercial success or, to use the vernacular, more 'money in the till'.

It was this thinking that led to the birth of what I call the 'Love' Grid. The 'Love' Grid is my way of explaining the link between the internal company behaviour, normally set by the bosses, and the consequential customer experience and customer relationship. As with much of my work, I first drew this up on a flip chart as a way of trying to land a point. Starting with the grid

Customer Experience	Company Behaviour	Customer Relationship

Fig. 9.1 The 'Love' Grid

Customer Experience	Company Behaviour	Customer Relationship
OK	Dealer Product and price	Transaction

Fig. 9.2   The 'Love' Grid (a)

itself, there are, in my opinion, three types of internal behaviour. None are essentially wrong but each has its consequences.

I will explain each one in turn, starting at the bottom and working my way up. The first is the 'Dealer' behaviour.

The Dealer behaviour happens when virtually the only discussion and focus of the leadership team is around 'product and price'. How are we going to sell the most product we can, at the best price we can get? When this conversation becomes the dominant one, and is in effect all the bosses worry about, it is no surprise that the rest of the employees follow suit. They become lost in a hard-nosed transactional behaviour with little thought or concern about the customer experience or the relationship the customer has with the company. They don't really care as long as the customer has spent some money. From the customer's perspective this means in effect: I go, I buy and I leave and have no emotional engagement with the company. There is no equity, no relationship, just the transaction. It's the customer equivalent of the 'one night stand'. It's what I feel when I go to WH Smith. I go, I buy my copy of *The Times* and leave politely, refusing the chocolate offered to me as a 'deal'.

There is nothing intrinsically wrong with this approach, except it leaves the company very blinkered and vulnerable to two issues. First, another company comes along with a better product or, second, a cheaper price, or potentially a combination of the two. As the customer has no equity with the original company they will almost certainly leave for the new company with the shinier offer and spend their money there. Of course the notion of dealing and trading has been around pretty much forever. The action or activity of buying and selling goods and services helps the world go round. What seems to have changed, especially since the financial crash, is that at the very time employees and customers want companies to have more of a sense of purpose, values and beliefs such as a Whole Foods or an IKEA, dealer behaviour has for many become the norm; particularly in UK retailing. For the last few years 'Product and Price' seems to have been the only game in town. All day and every day. Which by definition lessens the impact of a tailored promotion or the sale.

It was not always like this. Back in my BHS days we would have what was called a promotional calendar. This was partly made up of calendar events such as Christmas or Valentine's Day with the goal of creating some excitement in-store, and partly made up of times of the year when certain product ranges became more of a priority. 'Back to School' when children needed a new or replacement school uniform or 'Lighting' when the clocks went back. The logic being that it gets darker earlier in the evening, people switch on their lights and are more aware of the lighting in their home so they think about their lighting needs more. A bit like the Cherry Blossom season in Japan, this feeling is relatively short lived, so in order to maximise sales during the 'lighting season', a promotion would be created which was normally price led. Lighting was one of BHS's few real product strengths but at the very time in the year when lighting products came to the fore there would be a 20% off promotion. Whilst increasing sales in the short term in the following year, the start point was always to look at last year's figures. Lo and behold there was a peak in sales when the clocks went back driven largely by the deal. Which meant the only way to achieve this year's target was to run another 20% off event, and so it went on.

Price promotion is like a drug, and the more a company does it, the more addicted it becomes and the greater the difficultly to wean itself off. What starts off as a one-off ends up being the company strategy. I witnessed this as a customer of Threshers, the UK drinks retailer. What began as the occasional 3 for 2 offer over time became the norm. Then there was always a 3 for 2 offer, and if there wasn't one the customer had learnt to wait for the next one. With the only focus being price, training and product knowledge for the employees seemed to go out the window. There was little love or knowledge about the wines, beers and spirits being sold, and the whole experience, which given the category should at least have been an enjoyable one, was totally transactional for the employee and the customer. It usually spells the end when a customer will only spend money because of a deal, as was the case with Threshers. The company went into administration not long after in 2009.

When asked about this type of approach, and what went wrong, most bosses who have a 'dealer' mentality end up blaming somebody else. The weather, online, the supermarkets. Anything other than their own leadership.

In truth it is often laziness and a lack of ability and vision from those at the top. The focus on product and price is easy to do. It is tangible and measurable and the company pays little heed to what some find the tricky stuff: its people, culture, sense of purpose and what makes it different. In truth a company is either different or discount, so if it pays little attention to the former it becomes the latter. For a while it can work but rarely in the long term. Yet almost all of UK retailing is now gripped by dealer behaviour and a focus on just product and price, meaning most customers end up buying based on price alone. As a consequence UK retailing has largely sold its soul to the devil, and Oscar Wilde's phrase about a man who knows 'the price of every-thing and the value of nothing'[1] could not be more apt. Of course this con-stant focus on price also blunts one of the most effective instruments a retailer can have: their annual or bi-annual sale.

I was reminded of this when watching a programme called 'Inside Harrods' on Channel 5.[2] Back in the day, the Harrods Sale was a monumental event. The green and gold bags, now famous the world over, were introduced in 1935 and to begin with were only available during the Harrods Sale. Decades later in the 1980s it had become huge. The Harrods Sale would always start a week later than everybody else and never on Boxing Day, which used to be the norm. Supported by some iconic advertising and the latest must-have celeb-rity to open the first day. Always bang on time, for if one minute late, £17,000 worth of sales would be lost. Eleven million pounds would be in the till by the end of the day, which at the time was a world record. At its peak the Harrods Sale was something to look forward to, and customers would carefully plan their route to the goods they were after so that they would be first to get their hands on a bargain. Today, it has lost some of its lustre but it remains a big event.

Of course, other retailers in other countries use price promotions as part of their activities, but it seems that only in the UK and perhaps the USA has it become so dominant. Sales happen in Sydney, Singapore and Stockholm. Just not all day and every day!

It's not just retailing which has become dominated by 'Dealer' behaviour. In the countries I have worked in there is not much love but often a lot of hate for mobile phone network suppliers and almost all utilities. The primary rea-son for this is that with so much internal focus on the deal and signing people up, little attention is given to the actual experience of being a customer and specifically when something goes wrong. No company is perfect. Things go wrong. Customers largely accept that. It is how the company behaves in try-ing to sort out an issue that largely shows where it is on the 'Love' Grid. Heaven help you if something goes wrong with your BT landline or Broadband as it is like entering Dante's first circle of hell, which is 'Limbo', more commonly known as the call centre. Which is sad because when you finally get an engineer to come around, they are almost invariably really good and helpful.

In the summer of 2018, I had two transport-related challenges which illustrated how different companies react to a problem: at Heathrow and Eurotunnel. Dante's 'Limbo' rather neatly summed up the two experiences. The first involved getting our daughter, Sophie, checked in for her flight back to Sydney at Terminal 2. We got to Heathrow over three hours before the flight was due to take off, partly because she was taking her bike back with her and it needed to be cellophane wrapped. Much to my surprise, this part went remarkably smoothly. We then joined the queue for the Thai Airways Economy Check In. Accept it wasn't just for Thai but seemingly every flight out East that evening including China Airways and Singapore Airlines. There were a lot of people waiting to check in, and only one person doing the checking in. Being in a non-specific uniform suggested she was working for the airport rather an airline. Most people in the queue, including myself, stayed relatively calm, despite the limbo we seemed to be in as the queue had hardly moved in two hours. No airport representative seemed either to care or help. Stress and panic set in with an hour to go before the flight was due to take off. One extended family with what looked like over twenty pieces of luggage was taking forever to be checked in with still just the one person available. Miraculously, I saw a Thai Airways Customer Service person and with a shout and hand waving I was able to get his attention. Like some airport version of Moses and the Parting of the Red Sea he led us and the bike through the crowd to the now unused Thai Business Class check-in. Within ten minutes Sophie had been checked in and the bike deposited at the large baggage check-in and we had our tearful goodbyes. I turned to find our helpful man from Thai Airways to say thank you and noticed that the same family were still being checked in! I have no idea whether all the people waiting for their flights made it onto their respective planes.

A few days later, Karen and I were heading for a weekend in Montreuil in Northern France. We were on a relatively early train with Eurotunnel and as we were driving down we received a text warning of delays. Our trip coincided with extremely hot weather, which meant the air conditioning onboard the trains was struggling to cope, so Eurotunnel restricted the number of cars per carriage, meaning a backlog that grew and grew. We were back in another type of limbo and ended up with a four-hour delay. Leaving aside the small matter of the lack of investment in the trains, which are now starting to show their age and their inability to cope with hot weather, what was incredibly frustrating was the lack of communication. The information on the departure boards bore no relation to what was happening and there was no one around to ask who had any idea of when our allotted train was likely to depart. Anyway we got there and had a fabulous weekend, although frustratingly the journey back was not much better.

So I complained. Both to Heathrow and to Eurotunnel. What happened next was interesting. In all I had five emails back from Passenger Support @ Heathrow before I gave up. Like our politicians, they never really answered the question I was asking and kept passing the buck back to Thai Airways, despite the fact that, as you may recall, the check-in staff did not work for Thai or any other airline. So who did they work for? I had a little inside information having worked with the leadership teams of both Manchester Airport and East Midlands Airport so I know a third party, such as Swissport, may be used to handle the check-in. What was also curious about these emails back was the time they were sent. Two were within a minute of one another at 21.57 and 21.58 and the other two arrived at 20.20 and 20.27. All from the rather aptly named Suzii Steele. All of which led me to believe I was not dealing with an actual Suzii Steele but an artificial intelligence equivalent.

Suzii won, I gave up and the whole experience was unsatisfactory. In contrast, I received two emails from Eurotunnel. The first was to say that they would get back to me. The second was to say sorry and to offer a full refund. No quibble. I thought 'good on you' and we used the voucher within the month. Two responses. Two different behaviours. Shame on you, Heathrow.

So, is it possible to have a sustainable business operating with a 'Dealer' behaviour? In the short term yes but over the long term no. The customer will have no equity in the relationship and once something cheaper and/or better comes along then people will vote with their feet.

For quite a long time Ryanair would be held up to me as one example of a successful business with a 'Dealer' mentality and longevity. People know what they get with Ryanair. 'It will be awful but we know that and the fun starts when we get there'. For a good while this did hold true but I first started to hear about a backlash a couple of years back from people who had attended my Events, and more recently, it has run into a fair amount of turbulence. Almost all of it self-generated. Complaints about the lack of transparency over pricing when trying to book allied to a rejection of the 'cattle truck' flying experience have caused customers to reassess their view of Ryanair. Their employees also seem to be thinking again about their working environment and they too have had enough, with hundreds of flights cancelled and passengers hugely inconvenienced through their strike action in 2018 and 2019 to improve their working conditions. The profit warning in the autumn of 2018 and four months later in January 2019[3] was no real surprise.

Customer Experience	Company Behaviour	Customer Relationship
Enjoyable	Retailer Product and price Added value services	Respect
OK	Dealer Product and price	Transaction

Fig. 9.3 The 'Love' Grid (b)

In the middle of the 'Love' Grid is 'Retailer Behaviour'. This is not just about stores or retailing as such. What marks out this type of behaviour is the recognition that the company needs something more than just being solely reliant on 'product and price'. They believe they will need some sense of service mindset in their internal behaviour for them to be different and not discount. Just like an old-fashioned retailer. Once upon a time the middle seemed not only a safe place to be but the right place to be. The old adage 'Nobody gets fired for buying IBM'[4] was a homage to being risk-averse and doing largely what everybody else did. The phrase was equally applicable to Microsoft. Microsoft came to represent what IBM was: big, solid, reliable, reputable. The same would be said about Marks & Spencer in their pomp. Sensible clothes for sensible people from Middle England. Being in the middle meant appealing to lots of people. Bland maybe but with little risk of being seen as unusual.

I am not really sure when being in the middle was no longer okay. Perhaps we can thank Steve Jobs for this and the commercial which was used to launch the Macintosh back in 1984. 'Why 1984 Won't Be Like 1984' played on George Orwell's dystopian novel with the message that Apple was about freedom not control. It was directed by Ridley Scott of *Blade Runner* fame and it featured a rebellious young woman outrunning the Orwellian thought police and throwing a sledgehammer into a screen showing a mind-controlling speech by Big Brother. The long version of the commercial only ever ran once, at the Super Bowl.[5] This one airing had a massive impact. Not only did it launch the Macintosh, it changed the way people thought about computing. It also changed the way people, especially in the USA, thought of advertising.

It was named the 1980s commercial of the decade by *Advertising Age* and to this day still rides high in the 'best ever charts'. It established that Apple was different. Perhaps more than all of this, it challenged the myth that the middle was the right place to be.

However, 35 years on from 1984, the majority of business seems resolute in its attachment to the safety of the middle ground. I put this down to the rise of the career CEO and the influence of management consultants. I have nothing against CEOs who move around at frequent intervals or indeed people who work in management consulting. Good friends of mine such as Tony Barsham, who rather ironically works at IBM, are, or have been, management consultants. My experience though is that they tend to be very 'head' led. These CEOs are rarely trying to put a dent in the universe. They see themselves as there to do a job, which is well rewarded, and they focus more on the shareholder value than the customer experience. If successful after three years or so they move on. If unsuccessful, they still move on, often with their bonus intact. Their collective comfort blanket is data, analysis and strategy, which more often than not makes for a dry and risk-averse approach to business. They struggle with the human side of being a CEO.

They do recognise the need to have some sort of service ethos to differentiate them from the 'Dealer' approach, but the way they go about it means that because of this data-driven internal culture, the customer experience and the customer relationship end up lacking in warmth. The experience is better than okay, perhaps even enjoyable. The relationship is a lot more than just a transactional one and can lead to the company being respected. There is some equity created. A lot of airlines tend to end up here, particularly the 'flag carriers'. For many years I was a gold card holder of Star Alliance, as well as One World. This was largely down to the volume of trips I would take to the Nordics on SAS. I also used Lufthansa a fair amount when I had clients based in Germany. Almost every flight worked, be it in a very functional way. All was usually fine but I just didn't love the experience. The internal 'head-led' culture created an external 'head-led' experience.

Their biggest weak spot is that these companies measure their progress only against their category and rarely, if at all, against 'best in class'. Being in the middle and playing it safe is fine as long as nobody comes along and disrupts the company's universe. Kodak had 90% of photographic film sales as late as 1976 but became so obsessed with how they fared against their Japanese competitor, Fuji Film, that they completely missed the shift to digital and by 2012 had filed for Chapter 11 bankruptcy protection.[6] What Apple did to IBM Richard Branson did to British Airways with Virgin Atlantic. Until Virgin Atlantic came along British Airways was the only Britain-based airline flying the transatlantic, and whilst nowhere near as bad as what it has become today, it seemed complacent. Branson came along and began by taking the same identical product (a Boeing 747) but carving it up in a different way. His entrepreneurial flair mixed with his music business roots of Virgin Records meant that he saw things differently and always had an eye for making the customer experience just a little bit more memorable. Virgin Atlantic made flying long haul in economy fun rather than an experience to be endured. Better in-flight entertainment and ice cream on demand made the hours go by more quickly. Upper Class was a real innovation. I flew it on my first trip to Japan. There was no First Class and this was the Business Class offer positioned as a 'first class experience at a business class cost' complete with a chauffeur-driven pick-up and the original flat beds plus a cocktail bar on board all wrapped up in a slightly cheeky and maverick approach to service. I loved it.

Eventually British Airways had to take notice. However, as opposed to trying to compete on service, they launched their 'dirty tricks' campaign in an attempt to put Virgin Atlantic out of business. This included people from British Airways ringing up Virgin Atlantic passengers pretending to be from Virgin and saying that their flight had been delayed before switching them onto a British Airways flight. At the same time British Airways was feeding the press with false rumours about the financial situation of Virgin Atlantic. Branson sued for libel, using the services of George Carman QC. British Airways settled out of court when its lawyers discovered the lengths to which the company had gone in trying to kill off Virgin. They had to pay a legal bill of £3 million, damages to Branson of £500,000 and £110,000 to the airline. Branson donated the proceeds to his staff, calling it the 'British Airways Christmas Bonus'.[7]

Being safe and in the middle is not all it is cracked up to be. These companies may have all the analysis and data to hand yet rarely if ever do anything exciting or creative with it. Looking back at historical data and last year's numbers is helpful, but it is only ever part of the picture. If the CEO is more concerned with feeling smug with his or her tenure in the role than with the long-term health and well-being of the company, it does not prepare a company for change and the unexpected. Sometimes these changes are small and at other times seismic shifts happen, usually driven by some technological breakthrough.

The biggest of which in the last 20 years or so has been the internet. The company which has most successfully harnessed the power of the internet is of course Amazon. Amazon does not sit in the middle of the 'Love' Grid but has impacted virtually every business that does. Founded on 5 July 1994, some 10 years after the launch of Macintosh, its revenue in 2017 was close to $178 billion and employed over 566,000 people. In 2018 revenue was up 31% to $232.9 billion and it employed over 647,000.[8] This is remarkable growth by any standard. Its reach and scope pretty much touches all of us. What started with just books has morphed into a company which according to CNBC is forecast to own 49% of the total American online spending in 2018.[9] It is a business which is the epitome of 'Innovate. Constantly' for that is precisely what it does. It does not stand still for a second. It has shaken the business world to the core and largely for the better. Like any company which disrupts the norm, it is not without controversy, with employment conditions and tax issues to the fore, and time will tell whether its sheer scale and reach will provoke a backlash. Despite the massive growth, Amazon has not lost sight of the fact that the customer experience remains paramount to its success. It is not just about price but about the whole ordering experience, particularly when on the relatively rare occasion something goes wrong. It's hard to believe now but when Amazon first came along, we still lived in a world of mail order where it was not unusual for a product to arrive 28 days after the order was placed. Communication between the company and the customer was invariably poor and heaven help you if there was a problem and it had to be returned. My earliest memories of using Amazon was the shock of getting an email to say that the order would be delivered within two or three days. I seem to remember the order would always arrive before they said it would. Today, of course, everything is even more instant, with an order received less than a day after being placed. We do not have drone delivery in Gerrards Cross, but I guess that is only a matter of time. So there is still the human interaction of the delivery where sometimes something does go wrong. Very recently I ordered a book for my wife to take with her on a weekend break with her sister Laura Jane Sherwood-King, to Murcia in Spain. The book did not arrive even though I had notification it had. I contacted Amazon; once I had found the right form to fill and button to press, I had a reply within an hour to say that a replacement book was on its way. This one did arrive. Then, I had an email to say I would be charged for the first book as I had not returned it. Again the most complicated part of this was to find the right response section to explain my situation. Once found I emailed to confirm that I had not received the first book and therefore should not be charged. Within 30 minutes of sending this email I had received a reply saying, 'We are sorry for the inconvenience. It is certainly not what we expect our loyal customers to go through. To resolve this I've disabled the return requirement on the original item, as we know that you never received the product. And you won't be charged for your replacement order'. Compare that to the response I got from Heathrow.

So how on earth does a company respond to Amazon? Not by being in the middle or by being a 'Dealer' as to try to out-price Amazon is a recipe for disaster. The only way is to resort to those old-fashioned qualities of product knowledge, a good and eclectic range and a love for the subject matter. The perfect example of this is the Beachside Bookshop in Avalon on the Northern Beaches, outside Sydney, Australia. Avalon is a pretty cool place to stay. On the beach millennials really do go surfing and look drop-dead gorgeous as they sing and play their guitars as the sun sets. Teenagers eye one another up as they jump from the rocks into the waves, safe in the knowledge that they know all the rips, having been doing the same since they were nippers. Early mornings see lots of people, of all ages, out for a jog, doing some exercise or taking a swim in the open-air pool.

We had taken the bus from Sydney out to Avalon. The bus trip was an insightful one for me as I sat next to and behind a group of three young male Chinese tourists on their way to see where the series 'Home and Away' is filmed at Palm Beach. During the 90 minutes or so of the journey I was mesmerised by their dexterity on their respective iPads, switching from app to app and more impressively from English to Mandarin. Embracing knowledge and technology at the same time and giving me a brief insight into the output of the Chinese education system.

Five days of beachside living followed, including an almost record-breaking morning of 42C heat. All of which led us to want to buy an Aussie lifestyle book which would reflect our time there, and hence our visit to the Beachside Bookshop. It's a simple store that sells books. What made it different was the passion, knowledge and love of the owner and his team. Choosing the right

Customer Experience	Company Behaviour	Customer Relationship
Memorable	Brand Product & price Added-value services Sense of purpose Beliefs and values	Love
Enjoyable	Retailer Product and price Added value services	Respect
OK	Dealer Product and price	Transaction

Fig. 9.4 The 'Love' Grid (c)

book was almost like choosing a fine wine, with the discussion on the merits of the various books available, making the experience of buying a memorable one. I chatted to the owner about Amazon, which does not seem to be quite as massive over there as it is here. He was neither worried nor complacent. He knew his best way of surviving lay in their ability to curate the store, know their products and spend time with their customers. Plus have a simple to use online part of the business for those who wanted to use it.

Companies at the top of the 'Love' Grid simply go another way. They zig whilst everyone else zags. They behave as a Brand. This is not about branding. Brand behaviour is when the company is crystal clear in what makes it different. It understands its sense of purpose, values and beliefs to give clarity to its product, its price and its service offer, and in doing so, to make it unique. The CEOs who believe in this approach operate with a balance of 'heart' and 'head', but ultimately lead with the heart. They are often founders or entrepreneurial by nature. They work really hard with their people so that they are engaged and inspired about the company they work for. They know that if they get this right it creates the environment for their employees to love what they do and the company they work for. This energy and belief spills out. In turn leading to a customer relationship based on love and an experience which strives to be memorable. Visit any Cubitts store and you'll see what I mean. Their category of glasses and sunglasses has become commoditised. They have made their difference through having a flair for design and craftsmanship and having passionate employees who know what they are talking about. That is why for me there is an absolute connection between the mindset of creating memorable employee experiences which lead to memorable customer experiences and long-term commercial success. It puts the company culture at the centre of the business.

Hopefully, everyone reading this book will have a company or a customer experience they love. Be it a global company such as Apple or an independent bookshop such as Avalon's Beachside Bookshop. You might even work for such a company. Reaching and staying at the top of the 'Love' Grid is not easy, but the reward is great. Employees feel motivated because they feel loved, or as Warren Buffett puts it rather colourfully, 'There comes a time when you ought to start doing what you want. Take a job that you love. You will jump out of bed in the morning. I think you are out of your mind if you keep taking jobs that you don't like because you think it will look good on your resume. Isn't that a little like saving up sex for your old age?'[10]

There has been a whole new industry created around measuring the effects of employee engagement but I prefer these quotes to the numbers which can be found online. Steve Jobs had a lot to say on the matter: 'Your work is going to fill a large part of your life, and the only way to be truly satisfied is to do what you believe is great work. And the only way to do great work is to love what you do'.[11] Or as Quincy Jones believes, 'The people who make it to the top, whether they're musicians, or great chefs, or corporate honchos, are addicted to their calling. They are the ones who'd be doing whatever it is they love, even if it weren't being paid'.[12] Perhaps not surprisingly, one piece of advice I gave to my son and daughter, Oliver and Sophie, is that the most important aspect of work is to love what you do.

If employees love their company they become loyal and work not just harder but better. If customers love you, then they become loyal, they spend more money with you and they will recommend you to others. The 'recommendation of a company' has of course created a whole new measurement tool. The Net Promoter Score (NPS) developed by Fred Reichheld and Bain & Company and introduced in his 2003 Harvard Business Review article 'One Number You Need To Grow'.[13] It's a good measure and NPS has helped all of us who believe in the link between internal behaviours and the consequent financial success of the company to show that this is not airy fairy HR stuff but fundamental to the long-term health of the company.

It is one thing to be in love with the company but another to stay in love. Just like being in a marriage, this means staying attractive to one another, plenty of teamwork, listening to one another and tons of mutual respect. Just like being in a marriage, mistakes can be made, but can be forgiven. Being at the top of the 'Love' Grid means a lot of equity gets created amongst employees and customers. It gives the company some protection when something goes wrong. Those at Apple during its lost years around the mid-1990s and before the return of their founder put the very survival of the company down to the residual 'love' felt by the 'Mac User' group customers and some of the early employees…in spite of disagreeing with almost everything the company was doing at the time.

Ultimately, which of the three 'Love' Grid behaviours adopted internally is a choice. This almost always comes down to the leadership approach and ambition, attitude and skills of the boss. As I have said, each can work but they have their consequences. So my advice is to decide what suits and stick with it. The worst mistake a company can make, however, is to say they aspire to be at the top and behave as a 'Brand' whilst their actual behaviour is at the bottom behaving like a 'Dealer'. This is where leadership creates a problem for themselves. Greater transparency means it is a lot easier for both employees and customers to know how a company is really behaving. Saying one thing and doing another means there will be trouble ahead. This is where company values get a bad name. Almost every company will have its values on their website yet how many truly live up to them? Other than for the companies at the top of the 'Love' Grid, they are often generic, rarely authentic and not really believed in or lived by those at the top. If the boss and the leadership team don't live them, why should the employees?

As a customer I regularly experience these three types of behaviour. Whilst I will spend money with all of them, I spend the most with those at the top. This is not just my view but one shared by countless numbers of people across many countries who I know and have worked with in the past. Hence it is my belief that the rationale for The Business Case for Love is compelling and meets the needs of our times. Yet building a strong company based on love requires a modern, contemporary leadership style that embraces a new wave of thinking. Those who are stuck in their ways will find this a challenge. Those who are curious and seeking fresh insights and perspectives will feel invigorated and intuitively understand that to be sustainably successful every company needs their Company Spirit as its guiding light.

Notes

1. 'Oscar Wilde quotes', Goodreads, https://www.goodreads.com/quotes/390191-cecil-graham-what-is-a-cynic-lord-darlington-a-man
2. 'Inside Harrods: The World's Most Famous Department Store', Channel 5, 19 October 2018, https://www.channel5.com/episode/inside-harrods-the-worlds-most-famous-department-store/
3. 'Ryanair Profits Warning Due to "Lower Than Expected" Winter Fares', *The Independent*, 18 January 2019, https://www.independent.co.uk/travel/news-and-advice/ryanair-profits-warning-low-fares-loss-making-competitors-michael-o-leary-a8733886.html
4. '"Nobody Gets Fired for Buying IBM". But They Should'. *Forbes*, 30 November 2018, https://www.forbes.com/sites/duenablomstrom1/2018/11/30/nobody-gets-fired-for-buying-ibm-but-they-should/
5. 'How the Greatest Super Bowl Ad Ever – Apple's '1984' – Almost Didn't Make It to Air', *Business Insider*, 22 January 2014, https://www.businessinsider.com/apple-super-bowl-retrospective-2014-1
6. 'Kodak Files Chapter 11', *Forbes*, 19 January 2012 https://www.forbes.com/sites/ericsavitz/2012/01/19/kodak-files-chapter-11/
7. 'BA dirty tricks against Virgin cost £3m', BBC, http://news.bbc.co.uk/onthisday/hi/dates/stories/january/11/newsid_2520000/2520189.stm
8. 'Annual net revenue of Amazon from 2004 to 2018', Statista, https://www.statista.com/statistics/266282/annual-net-revenue-of-amazoncom/

9. 'Watch out, retailers. This is just how big Amazon is becoming', CNBC, 13 July 2018, https://www.cnbc.com/2018/07/12/amazon-to-take-almost-50-percent-of-us-e-commerce-market-by-years-end.html

10. 'Warren Buffett quotes', Goodreads, https://www.goodreads.com/quotes/380769-there-comes-a-time-when-you-ought-to-start-doing

11. 'Steve Jobs quotes' BrainyQuote, https://www.brainyquote.com/quotes/steve_jobs_416859

12. '17 Inspiring Quotes About Loving Your Work', Michael D. Pollock, https://www.michaeldpollock.com/inspiring-quotes-work-you-love/

13. 'The One Number You Need to Grow', *Harvard Business Review*, December 2003 issue, https://hbr.org/2003/12/the-one-number-you-need-to-grow

10

The Company Spirit

The vast majority of my work arises from two different business situations. Either the company has lost its way and the numbers are poor, so a new CEO has been appointed and the company needs to get clear again on what makes it different and what it stands for. Or, the company has a strategy in place but wants to add more 'heart' to the employee and customer experience. My work with, for example, Crew Clothing Company, Neverfail, West Cornwall Pasty Company and the Swedish bank SBAB fell into the former situation. My work with Swedish financial services company Lansforsakringar and East Midlands Airport was closer to the latter.

The four 'turn-around' companies could not have come from a more varied set of categories. Fashion, Food, Software and Banking, yet the similarities were remarkable. Three out of the four have had private equity involvement and the bank was government owned.

In the case of the three with private equity involvement, all had had either a founder or founders with an entrepreneurial streak. In their early days each was based around a strong product idea and their founders were trying, even in a small way, to put a dent in their respective universes. Intuitively they knew what made them different and generated a hard-working team-based culture around them. Although this was never written down they had, all in their own way, created their Company Spirit. Less a process, more a gut feeling as to what was right and wrong to do. They all grew, and along the way and at different times each attracted the attention of private equity. When investment is completed, the founders make some money and either leave soon afterwards or end up having a different, more advisory role. The new management team arrives with a brief of meeting the targets set by their

© The Author(s) 2020
M. Cox, *The Business Case for Love*, https://doi.org/10.1007/978-3-030-36426-7_10

respective private equity companies. I have nothing against any of this in principle. Yet with each business I became involved in, the company at some point started to unravel, the numbers turned sour and eventually, normally a year after they should have gone, the incumbent CEO was replaced and the new one arrived with the clock ticking to turn red numbers into black. So what goes wrong?

I may have an oversimplistic answer to this because there are often a myriad of reasons why a company loses its way, but I do put some of the blame on the private equity team and how they operate. When the courting is happening, there is a lot of due diligence to best understand the business they are investing in. This is almost always focussed on the tangible and 'head' aspects of the business and in particular the profit and loss accounts. Very little if any time is devoted to understanding the culture and the softer 'heart' parts of the business. Yet it was this very balance which had made each of these companies successful in the first place. The 'heart' and the 'head' operating in tandem. So when the founder leaves, a large part of the original spirit of the company leaves at the same time, the significance of which does not seem to bother or worry the investors at all. At first this does not seem to matter. The new team have been brought in for their management expertise not entrepreneurial zeal and they go about putting processes in place to improve the business. The 'head' takes over. Slowly, and to begin with imperceptibly, the culture changes and what was once clear becomes less so. Over time the company stops living any of the six 'Best in Class' company behaviours and it drops down the 'Love' Grid and becomes more transactional in nature. The spirit and the love get lost. The employees notice this first, particularly those involved from the beginning. Then the customers notice and start to question their loyalty. Then the figures go the wrong way, and after a year or so, the CEO is asked to leave and the new CEO arrives with the goal of reinvigorating the company and getting its Company Spirit back.

My other type of involvement happens when the boss and his or her team are clear about their strategy but sense that empathy, warmth and love are missing amongst their employees and their customers. They sit in the middle of the 'Love' Grid but with aspirations to move up to the top. So although the start points are different, the actual needs for these types of situations are similar. Cultural change is a marathon not a sprint and success comes not just from knowing which steps to take but the order in which to take them. The first part of the journey is to create confidence, belief and clarity around what the company stands for and to increase the level of emotional engagement employees feel with the company they work for. Experience has taught me that the most powerful way of doing this is not to start with the future but to begin by looking backwards to the birth of the company. To get under the skin of the ambitions, desires and energy which guided the original team by going back to the roots and to come to grips with how it behaved when it was at its best. No company is perfect. Each one has its ups and downs, and through sharing and listening to this story, the employees start to see the company in a different light. It becomes more real. More human. More authentic.

The origin of this approach was when I reflected on my time at BHS, and it was accelerated when at The Gathering. There were three projects which helped me crystallise my thinking, and the first of these, somewhat surprisingly, was our work with Kraft Foods and their brand Dairylea. For those who are unaware, Dairylea was originally packaged cheese triangles launched at a time when the UK was still experiencing rationing as a consequence of World War II. It was a quintessentially British brand made famous by a strong advertising heritage which won Dairylea a place in the hearts and stomachs of many a UK family. Nearly 50 years on from its original launch our involvement was to refresh the brand identity and packaging design. Back then, Kraft employed some really bright, inquisitive, highly personable marketeers and many went on to have very successful careers. Chris Priest was the Marketing Manager and I still see Chris to this day. I remember the team along with their advertising agency, JWT, having tons of research. Indeed perhaps too much because this tended to complicate rather than simplify their understanding. As is often the way, clarity gets lost over time and they wanted help to get everyone crystal clear on what Dairylea stood for. We went away with this team for a couple of days, which was a time, even today as I write, still memorable for me as it coincided with the general election and the subsequent arrival of Tony Blair as Prime Minister in May 1997. It heralded a new direction for the country and served as a monumental backdrop to our more prosaic search to unlock the success of these cheese triangles. Dairylea had a rich advertising history and we used this to understand and get clear on the roots. To try to imagine what it was like back in the early 1950s, and the role the brand went on to play in people's lives. Not the historical timeline, but how it behaved when at its best. It showed me the power of storytelling and how by looking backwards and inwards into the company, simplicity, clarity and authenticity can be created. We went on to work with many other Kraft brands amongst a wide range of other companies, and the start point with all of these was to go back to their roots. Not long afterwards Chris Priest moved to Gothenburg in Sweden to become Marketing Director of the potato chips and snacks company Estrella, and this became my introduction to working in the Nordics. Estrella was a Swedish brand, with its sister company Maarud in Norway. Both brands were owned at the time by Kraft, which had relatively recently launched Estrella in Denmark and Finland. The challenge Chris faced on arrival was that the four countries could not agree on the advertising approach, mainly because each country had its own view about what Estrella stood for. Our work was to unite the teams around a common language and understanding which would result in a communication brief everyone could agree on. Again, the answer was in the roots, although what was different for me was that in spite of the fact that Estrella was a 'packaged' brand, those involved were drawn from a much wider set of roles than just marketing. People from the factory, production and sales were involved. We were dealing with the entire company, and this sparked my real interest in the link between values, people and the culture of a company, not just values and communication. Having said that, we did create a unity amongst the marketing team, and The Gathering went on to create outstanding brand identities and designs for both Dairylea and Estrella as a consequence of this clarity, and I remain very proud of this work.

The third project was for Robert Bosch. I had first met Graham Ryan when he was General Manager of Dremel and then again when he moved to be European Director of Sales and Marketing at Bosch Power Tools. Graham was, and I am sure still is, a true gentleman. Looking back, Graham was one of the first people I had met who exemplified the idea of 'heart' and 'head' in their leadership approach. Again our work was to create clarity amongst disparate teams, with this time the axis being teams from Germany and the USA. With the greatest respect to the Dairylea and Estrella teams, the impact Robert Bosch and the company bearing his name had on the world was significantly larger, yet there were similarities, with the story of the man and the company somewhat lost. Sixty years after his death, Bosch the company came over as quite cold, known for excellent quality products and its engineering prowess, but not much love. The roots of the company could not have been more different. Robert Bosch was not only a superb engineer with great drive but also an empathetic entrepreneur. The James Dyson of his day. Bosch opened his first factory in Stuttgart in 1901 and the first sales office and first factory were opened in the USA in 1906 and 1910 respectively. By 1913, the company had branch operations in the USA, Asia, Africa and Australia and was generating nearly 90% of its sales outside of Germany. Just think about the logistics of this achievement. The travel, the language and cultural challenges he and those working for him must have faced.

It was, however, this human side of his approach to business which had got lost over time. When we were looking back at archival material we found that a big clue to his philosophy lay in the dramatic posters from the period either side of World War I. This was a time when the founder of a company would often sit down to brief a graphic designer. It led to posters which reflected Robert Bosch's view on what his company stood for. Bold artwork which dramatised how lives were saved and improved through Bosch products. He also had a strong sense of social responsibility and was one of the first industrialists to introduce the eight-hour working day. Later in life, he gifted a hospital to the city of Stuttgart in 1940. After his death, the company, on his instructions, was organised in such a way as to continue to donate earnings to charitable causes. It was this 'Making People's Lives Better' part of the roots which had been forgotten yet was a fundamental part of what made Robert Bosch, the man and the company, different. It was a prime example of a company which at the outset was at the very top of the top part of the 'Love' Grid and I like to think that those involved, primarily based at either Chicago or Stuttgart, learnt to love their company just a little bit more, because of truly experiencing the spirit Robert Bosch had as a founder.

Twenty years on from those heady days of the early reign of New Labour and Tony Blair, one of my big insights is how bad companies are at knowing, understanding and looking after their roots. Every company has a story to tell but all too often it forgets to tell it. It is dismissed as not important or relevant to the company's future. Yet understanding why a company was set up in the first place, and the hopes, dreams and aspirations of the founding team, is a wonderful experience. To come to grips with the ups and downs and to hear how the company behaved when doing well and not so well is powerful and engaging. Listening to the story puts the emphasis on the human side of the company. It truly touches the heart and is the foundation for an authentic company culture. This is the side which gets forgotten unless those at the top want to look after, care for and nurture the roots.

So when a company loses its way, and forgets its sense of purpose and what it stands for, the answer to how to get it back will be in the roots. This has been true with every single client of mine and perhaps is best illustrated by my work with SBAB, the Swedish bank. I first met Carl-Viggo Östlund, known to all as Viggo, over breakfast at my favourite Stockholm hotel, Berns. It was early December 2011 and it was very snowy and cold outside. It was to be my last meeting of a new business trip taking in Oslo and Stockholm. It was the one I was most looking forward to because although we were only connected via LinkedIn, his posts and comments were not what one would normally expect from the CEO of a bank. I did not know at the time of meeting that Viggo was essentially between jobs. Having finished his role as CEO at Nordnet Bank and about to start as CEO of SBAB. I also did not realise that Viggo was a close acquaintance of Mats Liedholm, who I had first worked with during the 'Kraft years' and who had subsequently become both a good friend and client on more than one occasion. Viggo embodied that sense of curiosity in my philosophy and approach which I look for in a potential client, so we connected immediately. I kicked off a project with him and his new team at SBAB soon after his arrival. SBAB was an online bank with a customer service centre which had lost its way. This was not due to private equity involvement, but rather the consequence of a change of direction. Once again the answer was to be found in the roots. SBAB's strength had been in mortgages, and when behaving at its best it really challenged the status quo, coming across as 'on the side of the people'. Helping them get a better mortgage, a better home and, as a consequence, a better life. The other bigger banks took notice and muscled their way into this territory and the SBAB response was to try to become a new type of bank rather than focus on updating their core strengths of being a mortgage lender so that it stayed relevant to the potential flat and house owners of today. The work I kicked off helped SBAB to get back to its roots and to create the mindset for a memorable customer experience for its customers. A mindset which, I have to say and judging by the continued behaviours of the traditional UK banks, is still pretty rare within the banking world!

The roots anchor the whole of the Company Spirit. They are by definition unique as no brand or company is the same. Each has its story to tell, and when told in a genuine, honest way, this means the Company Spirit is grounded in authenticity. One that will be recognised by long-standing employees and regular customers. It is this authenticity which starts to rebuild confidence, belief and love amongst the employees. With this in mind, let me introduce you to the whole Company Spirit model. It's what I call my signature dish, and my role is to help guide and facilitate its birth. Unlike many consultants, I start from the belief that the answer is in my client, not in me, and through the very act of creating their Company Spirit comes belief, ownership, clarity and a commitment to bring it to life. It kicks off cultural change (Fig. 10.1).

We create this as part of a two-day Company Spirit Event which normally involves all of the leadership team and a cross-section of employees. Once clear on the roots, those involved can start to think about and agree on the future of the company. 'Vision' is one of the most confusing and overused words in business. For simplicity, the way I help my clients to think about this is to view it from the perspective of the customer. In essence, what would you want them to say about your company in, say, a year's time? The 'passion' is essentially the everyday behaviour of the employees. A common language and understanding which employees get and customers feel. The bottom two

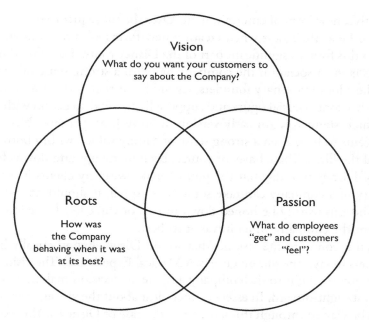

Fig. 10.1 The Company Spirit model

circles are the engine room, driving everyday life. The top circle is the flag at the top of the mountain: the direction of travel guiding behaviours and decisions.

The quick way I land this model with my clients is to use Disney as an example. Now let me be perfectly clear: I have never worked with or for any part of Disney. The following is not claiming to be the actual Disney Company Spirit, but an illustration of how the model works viewed from being a customer of Disney and some background reading. I use Disney as a way of explaining how the Company Spirit model works because wherever I am in the world people know and have experienced some part of the Disney Empire. They've watched a film or even been to a theme park, and the vast majority of those people have a strong emotional attachment to all things Disney. There are also some fabulous anecdotes associated with Disney.

In a similar way to Robert Bosch, it is easy to forget the impact Disney made in its early days, mainly because none of us were around to experience it first-hand. So when explaining how the Company Spirit model works in relation to Disney I try to transport my audience back to the time of silent movies. The 2011 film *The Artist* helps depict the impact that 'talkies' had on the audiences brought up only on silent movies, so when *Steam Boat Willie* arrives in 1928, it is not seen as a funny little cartoon but a completely innovative, new form of entertainment. Over the subsequent 90 years, Disney seems to be at their best when creating new forms of entertainment. In my opinion this forms a significant part of the Disney roots. The other dimension of roots is the association the company has with a strong sense of family values. Like a lot of visionary founders, legend has it that Walt Disney, the man, was both a controversial figure and supposedly not easy to get on with because of his high standards. An early version of Steve Jobs, perhaps. Nevertheless, there seems to have been a strong sense of 'family values' within both the studio and the films. There have, of course, been many ups and downs from the birth of Disney to today but the point I make with my clients is that whilst the story of a company can take some time to tell, it should not be complicated and can usually be honed down to two or three key behaviours which represent the company when it was at its best.

When it comes to the vision, what would Disney hypothetically like their customers to say? The phrase I use is 'A Magical Experience'. The vision should act as a guiding light to the company and create decision making that is simple and straightforward. In essence, once clear about the vision, every decision should be viewed through this lens. So in the case of Disney, is this experience we are talking about going to be magical for our customers? If it is, then do it and if not don't.

Passion is the employee part of the Company Spirit and acts as a crossover between how employees connect with their company. It's the everyday behaviour which employees get and customers feel. For Disney, I say this is 'Making People Happy'. I've always felt that it would be difficult to be a 'sad bugger' and work at Disney. Be it at the theme parks or working on their latest animated films, your personal values and company values really do need to align and one would need to be a happy soul, otherwise I think the experience would be pretty short-lived. It's also making people happy, not just children, as it is well known that part of the magic and enduring appeal of Disney has been their ability to appeal both to the parent and the child at the same time. Both ages connect at an emotional level, as witnessed by the well-reported fact that men, including the author, cry when watching *Toy Story 3*!

My view of what a Company Spirit for Disney could look like is shown in Fig. 10.2.

Just as the above hypothetical example shows, a real Company Spirit should be authentic and simple: inspiring to all the employees involved and creating clarity. Indeed I urge my clients to remember that once created, the answer is always in their Company Spirit. It enables any individual or team to say to themselves, 'Is what we are proposing going to feed and nurture our roots? Is it in line with our Passion and will it help get closer to our Vision?'

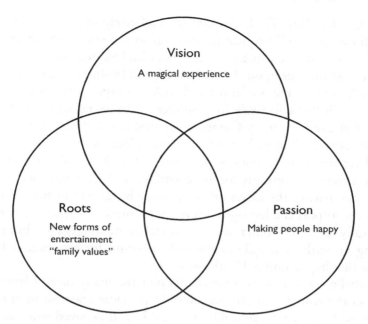

Fig. 10.2 The Company Spirit model as imagined for Disney

Every one of the 'roots stories' I have heard over the years since I founded The Company Spirit has been emotional. Some, such as when working with technology companies NXT and Imerge, recruitment company La Fosse Associates or Sweden-based coffee roasters Bergstrands, and very recently, Formech and Scicoustic, were particularly poignant as those involved the actual founder or member of the founding family telling their story. The latter involved the Vukovich brothers, David and Paul. With Bergstrands it was the two brothers Claes and Thomas Myren. With Crew I met with the founder, Alistair Parker-Swift, when Louise Barnes and I had dinner with him after the original Crew Clothing Company Spirit Event. We both had a good idea what the roots were, but were keen to double check with him, given that he had actually been there! Alistair got a bit annoyed with me because I said more than once that it was rare for me to meet the founder as they were usually dead!

Whether the founder is there or not, dead or alive, there is always the pro-verbial 'light bulb moment' when people suddenly realise what had made the company different in the first place. Sometimes it shows how simple behav-iours get forgotten in the quest for growth. The following four examples illus-trate this. First, the team at West Cornwall Pasty Company had effectively forgotten what was in their name and that a key part of their roots was taking pride in making a proper Cornish pasty. Second, when Martin Mackay took over as CEO at Neverfail he headed up a relatively small software company which for all sorts of historical reasons was spread over four offices, in three countries and two continents. Their roots highlighted that although their products had once been on the leading edge of business continuity they had fallen well behind. He was also faced with a company which given its geographical split had effectively four different cultures rather than one. Third, the roots of Crew Clothing Company stressed that a clear, simple and confident product offer had anchored a real sense of 'our crew' felt by early employees and customers alike. Fourth, the roots of East Midlands Airport featured a strong sense of community for those working at there. Customer service had always been part of the DNA, with the story being told of how in the early days of the airport the luggage handlers took pride in the suitcases not only being ready for the customers on their arrival in the baggage hall but each case standing up with its handle in the right position for easy access. Can you imagine that happening at Heathrow today?

The challenges for all of these clients plus the many more I have worked with over the years have been the same. To get clear again on what the company stood for, what made it different and how it behaved when at its best. Once identified, how to make their roots modern and relevant to the needs of today's business environment and customers?. How to use the Company Spirit to be the basis for a strong culture and create the mindset of memorable employee and customer experiences? How to do this in a way which engages the whole company so that each and every employee feels that they are clear on what their company stands for, and feel involved, inspired and accountable for bringing this to life through their role? How to measure, review and reward employees who live and breathe their Company Spirit? What to do about those who can't or will not live it? And for the CEO and the leadership team, how to behave as a 'Best in Class' leader and live the Company Spirit every day? In short, how to find love and stay in love.

These are the themes we will explore in Part III.

Part III

Staying in Love

11

How the Boss Can Be Loved

Once upon a time, most leaders knew that that they would be quite literally 'on stage' at some point during the year. Be it addressing the Sales Conference, announcing the Annual Results to their stakeholders and shareholders, or making the keynote speech at a supplier conference or product launch. Whether they loved or hated the experience, most took the view that this came as part of their job, and for the less confident, at least it happened only a few times a year.

Today, being 'on stage' has taken a very different meaning, as leaders are now on stage all the time. All day and every day. Their actions and behaviours, big and small, are scrutinised by the media and many are found wanting. Sir Philip Green seemed happy enough to be shown with his arms around Kate Moss, or at the front row of London Fashion Week. Less so when accused of alleged bullying and sexual harassment.[1] Jeff Fairburn was happy enough to take the money but his refusal to answer questions about his £75 million bonus when asked by Spencer Stokes for 'BBC Look North'[2] apparently cost him his job as CEO. His bonus and failure to answer questions about it was damaging the reputation of his company, Persimmon. No hiding place either for the directors of Carillion, which became the largest ever trading liquidation in the UK early in 2018, and subject to investigations by multiple Parliamentary select committees. The final report of the Parliamentary inquiry by the Business and Work and Pensions Select Committee opened with the words 'Carillion's rise and spectacular fall was a story or recklessness, hubris and greed…Even as the company very publicly began to unravel, the board was concerned with increasing and protecting generous executive bonuses.

© The Author(s) 2020
M. Cox, *The Business Case for Love*, https://doi.org/10.1007/978-3-030-36426-7_11

Carillion was unsustainable. The mystery is not that it collapsed, but that it lasted so long'.[3]

Shareholders rarely seem to hold the executive team to account, certainly not over pay and bonuses. Looking from the outside in, it seems impossible to justify how leaders are so often rewarded for failure. The disconnect between the payment of £8.3 million since November 2014 to Peter Fankhauser, CEO of Thomas Cook, and the non-payment to ordinary employees of the company for their final month's work is beyond belief. When asked about his salary, Fankhauser defended his pay, saying it was not 'outrageous' when compared to other bosses in the FTSE 250.[4] He also said packages had been set by the firm's remuneration committee and approved by, you guessed it, their shareholders. This lack of accountability and what appears to be collusion by various boards and board members by not asking too many difficult questions is not helping the reputation of business. Holding these bosses to account now seems to be the prerogative of the media, not the shareholders. Or, in extreme cases, Parliament.

The one group that will be extremely aware of how their bosses behave are their employees. Leaders who are 'loved' by their employees are constantly aware of their actions and behaviours. They are 'in the moment' reacting to what is happening then and there. They are always looking for ways of sharing news with their teams. Updating them on what is happening within the company in a natural and authentic way. They recognise that this cannot be faked or scripted. Fake it and in today's social media world the person will be quickly found out.

Old school bosses don't seem to understand this, and seem happy to say one thing and do another within the company they run. Completely oblivious to the effect this can have on those working for them. They fail to grasp that this behaviour plants doubt amongst their employees, who will quickly start to worry about whether to trust and believe what their boss says and does. Which, according to those who worked there, was precisely what happened at Thomas Cook.

In Chaps. 7 and 8 we have explored how to behave as a 'Best in Class' company. One which creates love amongst their employees and customers. This of course requires the boss to behave as a 'Best in Class' and modern-day leader. In this chapter I will focus on what this means. As with company behaviours, I believe there are six leadership behaviours which separate the best from the rest. Unsurprisingly, they are the complete opposite to those who operate with a command and control approach or whose primary driver is 'I' not 'we'.

Giving Not Taking

Any loving and sustainable relationship, whether at work or at home, requires the ability to give and take. Yet, 'old school' leaders traditionally only take. They take the credit for a team's effort. They take their employees for granted, and their customers for a ride. They take for themselves. They take the most money. They lack empathy and are often not very nice people. They thrive on being part of a macho culture and are very 'head led', believing a motivational speech should be no more than 'How many times do I need to tell you to just do it?' These are the behaviours I hear described by employees who have worked for this type of CEO. I listen to these stories after this person has been fired for the poor performance of the company. They describe behaviour not unlike that of the class bully. It is little consolation that this abusive behaviour often masks someone fundamentally insecure in their own ability. Constantly worrying that they will be found out.

'Old school' does not mean old. The 2017 ousting of Uber founder and CEO Travis Kalanick shone an unfavourable light not just on the culture he created at Uber, but on how the culture at many Silicon Valley companies was not always sweetness and light. As Anna Weiner remarked at the time in *The New Yorker*,

> Among my acquaintances in the tech industry, there's abundant Schadenfruede about Uber's fall from grace, but also a sense of uneasiness. The company is like the over-served cousin at the family wedding, the one who does the Running Man and sets fire to the centrepieces…not the representative you'd choose, but your DNA is undeniable.[5]

So this is not about age but rather attitude. Cool, trendy tech companies can also suffer from what for many seems an anachronistic approach to leadership. The need for speed, growth and rapid returns undoubtedly shapes the behaviour of the bosses and the consequent company culture. What was once a fun place to work gets overtaken by the need to hit the numbers. The mindset of wanting to create a memorable employee and customer experience is no longer prevalent. Perhaps everyone is blinded by the short-term money to be made and the bonus culture for those involved. Increasingly though, there is no hiding place for those who just take or behave in an abusive way. Ultimately, they are found out.

One of the many low points that the reputation of British business, and in this case businessmen, has brought upon itself was the portrayal of just what went on at The Presidents Club charity dinner held at The Dorchester in

London in January 2018. A men-only 'black tie' charity event exposed by an underground female journalist, from *The Financial Times*, hired to be a waitress for the night. What happened was given prominence on the front page. Describing the behaviour of the supposedly great and the good with tales of sexual harassment to the fore. The lead journalist, Madison Marriage, reported that waitresses were subject to groping and lewd comments. Some were questioned whether they were prostitutes, and whether they would join guests in their rooms.[6]

As the repercussions of this tawdry event rippled on through the British media, the death was announced of one of Sweden's greatest businessmen, Ingvar Kamprad. The founder of IKEA. The irony was not lost on me. He was a man who personified 'giving not taking'. For him 'giving' was about having a generosity of spirit. To be generous with time, and spend time listening to the concerns, ideas and worries of your employees. As this quote from his obituary in *The Times*[7] makes clear, he really wanted to improve the way people lived: 'I see my task as serving the majority of people. How do you find out what they want, how do you serve them? My answer is to stay close to ordinary people, because at heart I am one of them'. Kamprad's philosophy is perhaps best captured in his own 'Furniture Dealer's Testament', sometimes known as the gospel according to IKEA. Its maxims include 'waste of resources is a mortal sin at IKEA' and 'happiness is not to reach one's goal but to be on the way'. So not just a visionary man but a man with a clear sense of purpose, beliefs and values. This was a leader who created a company that changed the way people thought about design. Influencing for the better the way we lived and also loved, as apparently 10% of all Europeans were conceived on an IKEA bed!

Kamprad's approach to business could not be further removed from the behaviour of some at The Presidents Club, and the short-term, 'me first' approach of those at Carillion. Businessmen do not have to behave badly to succeed.

The Presidents Club was disbanded in the aftermath of the scandal. Thankfully it is the life-changing legacy of Ingvar Kamprad which will live much longer in the memory. It should shape the behaviour of any leader who aspires to create their own sustainable company.

Be Self-Aware

Listening to employees who have remained at the company following a change of leadership always reveals some fascinating insights. If this change is the result of the company getting into trouble, people are quick to pass comments on the failures of the old regime. Strikingly, they will always talk about how their previous boss became less and less of a team player. Indeed the worse the numbers became the more the CEO will rely on his or her own judgement or that of a very small inner cartel. There is little attempt to reach out to the broader team, in order to work together, to change the company's fortunes.

When the incoming CEO arrives, their start point will be to put together their team. The majority I have worked with give the existing leadership team the benefit of the doubt, at least to begin with, to see whether they can adapt to the new approach. Sometimes, and a bit like the football manager who brings their own backroom staff, CEOs will arrive with two or three loyal staff and the new and the old have to be united over time.

Building a winning team is neither easy nor quick, and in my experience the best CEOs often look to sport for their inspiration. A successful sports team is one made up of people who will have different yet complementary skills, who play together for the glory of the team, not the success of the individual. The role of the manager is to understand each member's own strengths and weaknesses, so they play together in harmony and for the common good. To be truly successful, the manager must also be self-aware. To understand their own strengths and weaknesses so that their coaching staff also operate in balance. It is the same in business.

To illustrate this point, those of you from the UK and of a certain age will remember the success of Brian Clough and Peter Taylor. The Football Manager and his sidekick. Together they achieved huge success in football, winning 'The League', first with Derby County in the 1970s and then with Nottingham Forest. This team also went on to win two European Cups. When they were individual managers, they had nowhere near the same success. Deep down they knew that they were better together, as they complemented one another. One was the 'loud mouth', the other the 'quiet man'. They were a team who created two successful teams.

A decade earlier, The Beatles were in their prime. John Lennon, Paul McCartney, George Harrison and Ringo Starr. Four people who when they were together made a huge impact on a generation's music and cultural tastes. Whose power is very much in evidence today. The 'Fab Four' were just that, a team. They certainly influenced Steve Jobs, who stated, 'My model for business is The Beatles. They were four guys who kept each other's kind of negatives tendencies in check. They balanced each other, and the total was greater than the sum of the parts. That's how I see business: great things in business are never done by one person, they're done by a team of people'.[8]

Notwithstanding the success of South Africa and the heroics of England at the 2019 Rugby World Cup in Japan, for me the best and most consistent sports team in the world is the All Blacks, the New Zealand Rugby Team. I have been privileged to see them play twice: in the quarter-final and the semi-final of the 2015 Rugby World Cup. England had already been knocked out, and I have to confess I became a bit of a fake and donned the black rugby shirt with the iconic silver fern for our trip to Cardiff for the quarter-final match against France. My excuse was that my daughter Sophie had just returned to the UK following her ski instructor training at Treble Cone, on New Zealand's South Island. A tenuous link, I know, and I was made to pay for it through the wit and sarcasm of the Irish supporters sitting behind me, once they knew I was English masquerading as a Kiwi.

During the match against France I witnessed the best rugby I have ever seen played. What makes the All Blacks different is not just their ability to play rugby, but the behaviour and the spirit of the team, which makes them such a beacon of learning for the business world. When one of England's finest, Jonny Wilkinson (the man who dropped the winning goal when England beat Australia to win the World Cup in 2003) was asked on TV about what made the All Blacks different, he didn't just talk about speed, agility, brawn or even clear thinking under pressure. He talked first and foremost about their behaviour, their culture and their values. That they are truly self-aware as individuals, and as a group, of their responsibility to honour the spirit of the All Blacks. Three examples around the time of the 2015 World Cup personified this.

First, as a team, their post-match protocol is to show respect to the opposition, by inviting them into their dressing room after the match. To foster a sense of fraternity and shared experiences in what the French call the 'third half'. To put aside the two halves of the match to acknowledge that everyone involved is chasing the same dream and is united by the same beliefs.

Second, as an individual, when Sonny Bill Williams famously 'gifted' his winner's medal to 14-year-old Charlie Line. The boy had been rugby tackled by an overzealous security guard as the team enjoyed their lap of honour following their World Cup victory, an award which had taken a lifetime of dedication to earn, and seconds to give away. An act which was both gracious and humble.

Finally, some of the players took a detour from their celebration tour of New Zealand to take the Webb Ellis Cup to the grave of a recent teammate, Jerry Collins, who had died in a car crash in France the year previously so that he could 'share' in the experience of winning the cup.

Characteristics which exemplify how a large part of the success of the All Blacks is through an understanding of the link between the self-awareness of an individual and the creation of a successful team. In my mind that is a pretty good reference point for those aspiring to do the same within business.

Goal Orientated, Not Task Orientated

A failure of many leaders is not understanding the difference between goals and tasks. They are subsumed in the day to day. They end up spending their life in meetings, sending and receiving emails, and ticking off the tasks on their 'to do' list. The 'task-led' mentality takes over, and the task becomes the goal.

This behaviour was brought home to me with absolute clarity in a discussion with a member of the leadership team at McLaren Automotive. Dick Glover had joined from the Formula 1 side of the operation and was the Technical Director at the time I was involved. He absolutely knew the difference between the two. As he explained, with a race every two weeks during the F1 season, the goal was to win the next race, and the tasks were the hundreds of individual jobs to help achieve the goal. The deadline for finishing these tasks was when the chequered flag goes down, and the race commences. Simple to understand and motivational for all those involved. Yet business leaders are often guilty of failing to do this. They will spend a lot of time crafting their strategic goals and the plan to get them there. However, during the following days or weeks, they often forget about the goal, and just focus on the tasks. They stop being a leader and become a manager instead. Politicians are particularly prone to this. It's the difference between Donald Trump and Theresa May.

Now I am not saying I particularly like, admire or agree with what Donald Trump says and does, but he has a very clear goal. To Make America Great Again. Viewed from this side of the Atlantic almost every task of his presidency is aimed at meeting this goal. Over here, Theresa May's equivalent was 'Brexit means Brexit', yet this became a slogan rather than a goal because no one within her government really agreed on what it meant. From the outside looking in, she seemed to want to manage the situation, rather than to lead it. Any vision as to what the UK would be, post Brexit, got lost. The tasks associated with leaving the EU completely took over her narrative, leaving the electorate frustrated, confused, exhausted and worried in roughly equal measure. Boris Johnson, having replaced Theresa May, had the very clear goal of 'We will leave on the 31st October, Do or Die', now morphed into 'Let's Get Brexit Done'. Jo Swinson, the now ex leader of centrist party the Liberal Democrats, also had a clear goal, but in the opposite direction. Jeremy Corbyn, as leader of the Labour Party, seemed to believe that the less clear he was on Brexit, the better.

I admit it is a bit of a leap to go from the presidency of Donald Trump and Brexit to Christmas trading at Crew Clothing Co. but the principles of leadership vs management and goal vs task remain the same. One of my last areas of involvement with the Crew team was with the Commercial Director, Dan O'Callaghan, and his Regional Team working with each of their store managers. Christmas is usually the biggest sales period for many retailers, and Crew were no different. Our goal was to try to change the mindset of the store managers from being task orientated to goal orientated. For them it is the busiest time of the year and there are many, many tasks. Our equivalent to the McLaren Racing goal of winning the next race was 'Let's make it the best Christmas ever', and the role of the managers was to keep them and their teams focussed on this goal through creating as memorable an employee and customer experience as possible. Simple, but it worked, as the teams knew why they were doing the tasks, and how they fitted in with the overall goal.

Staying focussed on the goal is a mindset. It separates out leaders from managers and winners from losers. In Chap. 9, I introduced the idea of the 'Love' Grid and in my experience leaders who aspire for their company to be at the top of the 'Love' Grid really do understand the difference between goals and tasks. Those who run companies in the middle of the 'Love' Grid are less clear. They 'lead' by managing the tasks and feel happiest with finding the step-by step solution required to meet objectives, often forgetting what the original goal was along the way. Something Donald Trump or Boris Johnson cannot be accused of.

Communicate to Engage. Tell Stories

'The PowerPoint Presentation'. Three words which instil dread in those about to witness it and those about to give it. The phrase has become synonymous with boring presentations. It made people lazy. Ill-thought-out presentations with far too many words on each page, delivered in a monotone voice with the 'presenter' often just reading out what had been written on the page. Usually shown with the lights turned down, exacerbating boredom and sometimes inducing sleep for those attending. Complicating what should be simple. It de-humanises the art of communication.

The expression 'less is more' is the natural opposite to this state. First used in 1855 as part of the Robert Browning poem 'Andrea del Sarto', it gained greater prominence after being adopted by architect Ludwig Mies van der Rohe in 1947.[9] Used to describe minimalist design and architecture, it is now in common parlance. It also reflects what most of us feel. When we are clear and confident, we simplify, not complicate. Indeed the more confident we are in the message, the less wordy it will be. This was the mantra of New Zealand-born Andrew Niccol, the best advertising copywriter I have had the privilege to work with, and who went on to make it in Hollywood as the writer of *The Truman Show*, and to write and direct many films. Andrew was instrumental in the creation of the most impactful campaigns I have worked on. Madame Tussauds and the launch of Philips Compact Disc were the best examples. I can remember, as if it were yesterday, sitting in his office whilst he would agonise over making sure the headline and the copy were as succinct and sharp as possible.

Andrew knew that successful copywriting and directing, whether for a 60-second commercial or a feature-length film, was all about storytelling, and that is how the best leaders talk. They communicate to engage. They tell the story but make you, the audience, their employees and their customers, part of the story. Steve Jobs was, of course, the pass master at storytelling and his product launches at MacWorld are legendary. Talking without notes in a natural and human way using sharp, distinct messages on screen to aid the presentation.

It is the style that most employees would like their bosses to adopt. They certainly do not take kindly to being lectured at, creating a sense of us and them. I witnessed this in person when I was involved in a conference at RBS a year or so before the Financial Crash. It was a disaster. The atmosphere in the room was quite febrile. Every so often various recorded 'Big Brother'-type messages from the bosses were played out on screen to the audience of a hundred or so. It really did feel like George Orwell's *1984*.

Halfway through the day, one of the bosses came and gave a pep talk to the assembled employees. This man was arrogance personified. A shortish man, sweating away in an ill-fitting if expensive suit. Strutting up and down in front of the employees talking about the success of RBS and how it behaved like a 'restless shark', hoovering up companies, people and business to become ever more successful. Fred Goodwin was praised as the Sun God. This made me feel distinctly uneasy. Although I did not know it at the time, this was a glimpse into the corporate culture of RBS. One of avarice and hubris. A year or so later, the bank all but collapsed, and the 2008 annual loss of £24.1 billion[10] was the largest in UK corporate history.

The summer of 2007 saw the launch of the first iPhone, with a style and approach a world away from my RBS experience. At about this time RBS and Apple had a broadly similar market capitalisation. However, a decade or so on, there is a gulf between the levels of success of the two companies. In November 2019, RBS had a market capitalisation of £23.71 billion.[11] Apple meanwhile stood at $1.14 trillion.[12]

The differing styles offered up by those at Apple and those at RBS show how communication was a reflection of the corporate culture prevalent at that time. Today's employees will not put up with being shouted at. Less is more. They want simple, clear messages shared in a compelling way and, preferably, without a PowerPoint being involved.

Be Curious

Not everyone will love what they do or the company they work for, and there will be a myriad of reasons why this is the case. I find it sad, however, when I come across people who seem to be just going through the motions of being at work. One of my clients, Dr. Bruce Macaulay, used to call these people 'the frozen middle layer', and I always thought this was quite an apt description as more often than not they were men, approaching their middle years and in middle management, who had sort of given up. I still see this term a lot when I talk to people as part of my Discovery and this is not just the preserve of men. Perhaps this is part of what we mean by a 'mid-life' crisis. The characteristics of those in the frozen middle layer are often a combination of going through the motions at work and a tendency to be critical, usually behind their backs, of those people who are full of energy and trying to do their best. These people seem to have ended up weighed down by life. The mortgage, family responsibilities, perhaps a marriage or relationship which is not going to plan. The energy and excitement of their twenties and early thirties seems to have got lost and work becomes something to be endured, not loved. They are often described as cynics, although I disagree. The cynics I have come across, and there have been many, often really do care about what is happening, but have become frustrated by poor leadership and decision making and tend to be quite vocal about it. These people remain curious but just have a funny way of showing it.

I came across this frozen middle layer when I ran my initial Discovery at Lansforsakringar, in Sweden. I was working with the team at their Maklarservice non-life insurance division, and with their leader at the time Peter Griepenkerl Loof. I had first met Peter a few weeks earlier and we just clicked. Peter had a strategy in place but was looking to add more 'heart' to both the employee and customer experience. To make it less transactional. Neither the team nor the division was in crisis. There was no burning platform to change, and when

I started my Discovery I was not sure what I would find or what insights I would uncover. Discovery is essentially a series of one-on-one conversations where I listen to people sharing their thoughts on everyday life at the company they work for. There are no formal questions, as I like to let the conversation follow its natural course. As a stream finds the best way to flow downhill. I try to talk to as wide a range of employees as possible, covering different ages, responsibilities and lengths of time with the company. I liken this to a jigsaw puzzle as gradually through these conversations I get a clear picture of how it feels to work there. In this case I was struggling a little to get a sense of what people felt, but the more conversations I was having the more I felt that, although there were a couple of cynics, there were two distinct groups of people working at Lansforsakringar Maklarservice. I named them the 'cool' people and the 'canteen' people.

The 'cool' people were full of energy, interest and curiosity. Leaning forward into the conversation and eager to share their views and learn more about my approach. The 'canteen' people were more reticent to engage. They liked meeting up at the canteen for lunch with their friends and then a couple of hours later for a fika (a Swedish tradition of a coffee and cake). These employees were not disruptive but were no longer curious or open to fresh ideas and perspectives. They carried out their job in a professional manner but came across as happy with the status quo. They did not mind coming to work but did not 'love it' in the same way that the 'cool' people did. When I fed this insight, amongst others, back to Peter and his leadership team, they readily concurred and also understood that unless the situation changed, the energy would be sapped from the 'cool' people who in turn could get frustrated and then leave.

Whilst this can be frustrating for those involved, this is not as bad as when this lack of curiosity and energy extends to those who are involved in any leadership team and certainly if it effects the boss. To be a 'Best in Class' leader, the individual at the top has to have the ability to inspire, energise and excite their teams, and this is almost impossible to achieve authentically if the person is not inspired themselves. Yet this is what happens. People get to the top but the battle to get there has exhausted them. They became inward facing, talking to and involving their 'inner court' of confidants rather than getting out from behind their desks to explore what's new. They do the job, but don't love doing it, and it shows.

Each and every one of the CEOs I have worked with over the last few years has been curious. This manifests itself in different ways. Some read a lot or have eclectic taste in music. Others go out of their way to visit new places, be it the latest restaurant or a country they have not been to. Peter G.L. (as he is known for short) has since moved on to a different role in Lansforsakringar. He founded in parallel the idea of 'Management by Art' to help inspire better leadership through an appreciation of art. Martin Mackay upped sticks to work in Singapore and the Far East with all the challenges and excitement that brings, embracing and thriving on the different cultures and people he came across. Carl-Viggo Östlund regularly updates his Instagram page with the latest book he is reading. Mats Liedholm, now with a new role as MD of Fazer Lifestyle Foods, is well travelled but wants different experiences. Visiting new countries on holiday or insisting on taking me to a recently opened restaurant. Frank Stephenson, who was Design Director at McLaren Automotive, having previously designed many of today's most iconic current cars including the Mini, the Fiat 500 and Ferrari F430, had a sailfish, one of the fastest fish in the world, on his wall when I first met him. This was symbolic of his own curiosity. He explained to me how understanding how the sailfish could achieve such speeds became a start point for the design of the texture of the ducts that lead into the engine of the P1 Hypercar. He went on to explain how he was influenced by nature's ability to create amazing creatures, and by haute couture's tendency to shock and push the boundaries. These are some of his start points for car designs. Frank personifies more than most the notion of 'be curious' as a behaviour which leads to groundbreaking design and commercial success. I hope the reader can tell that I am enormously influenced by the experiences I have. One of the joys of what I do is meeting and working with very different people and companies in a range of different categories and cities around the world. It's through these experiences that I try to keep myself fresh. We all, of course, can get stuck in a rut, which is precisely why I find it so important to let curiosity get the better of me and to try to constantly explore new ideas. Even though I am chided, particularly by Mats Liedholm, for always staying at the same hotel when in Stockholm.

Heart, Then Head

The 'Love' Grid shows the link between the internal company behaviour and the external customer experience and customer relationship and the choices a company can make. The leadership 'Love' Grid has a similar format, this time showing the link between leadership behaviour, the employee experience and the employee relationship. There are again three types of behaviour and each one has its consequence. As before, we'll start at the bottom and

Employee Experience	Leadership Behaviour	Employee Relationship
OK	Dealer Head Lead "Just Do It!" Tell	Transaction

Fig. 11.1   The leadership 'Love' Grid (a)

work upwards. I've covered quite a lot of these points already so think of this grid as a summary.

The 'Dealer' approach to Leadership is completely 'head' led and involves a lot of telling people to 'just do it'. It's the most old-fashioned of the three and has its roots in the command and control approach to business, which, in essence, is 'I'm the boss, get on and do as I tell you'. It dates from the Industrial Revolution when people were recruited to work in factories for long hours with little pay and brutal conditions. All the while patrolled by the 'boss' whose management style would be fear and loathing. These 'sweatshop' conditions still exist today and are often associated with the clothing industry in India, China, Indonesia and Vietnam. Whilst the 'sweatshops' have largely disappeared from the 'West', the leadership style perseveres. No longer just the preserve of factories, it remains the leadership style of choice for many whose primary focus is 'I' not 'we'. The consequence of this approach is an employee experience which is no more than 'okay' and a relationship they have with their boss and the company which is transactional: 'I go to work to earn money and that's all I get from it'. What has changed in the West and is rapidly changing in the East is that employees have more of a choice as to where they work. If the employee has next to no loyalty, due to the behaviour of the boss, and does not feel valued they will be on a constant lookout to change jobs. Short term, there is only one winner from this 'Dealer' approach and that is the person in charge. However, in today's business environment this is rarely a sustainable successful strategy.

Employee Experience	Leadership Behaviour	Employee Relationship
Memorable		Love
Enjoyable	Retailer Head then Heart 'Please contribute to it' Shape	Respect
OK	Dealer Head Lead "Just Do It!" Tell	Transaction

Fig. 11.2 The leadership 'Love' Grid (b)

Employee Experience	Leadership Behaviour	Employee Relationship
Memorable	Brand Heart and Head 'Let's create it together' Share	Love
Enjoyable	Retailer Head then Heart 'Please contribute to it' Shape	Respect
OK	Dealer Head Lead "Just Do It!" Tell	Transaction

Fig. 11.3 The leadership 'Love' Grid (c)

The next one up is 'Retailer'. It is an apt description for this approach to Leadership as most retail bosses tend to be 'task led' not 'goal led'. Opting for a more managerial way of leading. For the majority of employees though, it is infinitely better to work with this type of boss than the 'Dealer' approach. At least there is usually some attempt to involve people in the development of the company. There is some emotional involvement but it remains very much led by the 'head'. Here engagement translates to the once or perhaps twice a year 'Company' meeting and weekly email. People are updated on what is happening in the company and encouraged to have input. This is the world of the professional manager. They understand that the 'Dealer' approach is poor for the employee experience because they have been on enough business courses to know better. In the middle is where we will find the majority of leaders who have an MBA. Super bright people who are happier with their PowerPoints and their spreadsheets and struggle with the human side of the business. The best ones can elicit respect from their employees and at least understand the importance of an experience that employees enjoy.

As with the Company 'Love' Grid, those leaders at the top who exhibit 'Brand' behaviour just go another way. They fundamentally understand the needs and desires of what the majority of people are looking for in 2019 and beyond, from their employee experience. Today most employees reject, if they can, the 'Dealer' approach. Employees can live with the 'Retailer' approach but, in my experience and not surprisingly, would prefer to work for and be led by someone who truly believes in 'we' not 'I'. A leader who offers a combination of clarity and involvement and wants to create an environment where people work together to share the approach and build the company as a team. A leader who listens, is empathetic and works hard in trying to create the right environment for people to reach their full potential. One who leads with the 'heart' and follows with the 'head'. These people absolutely understand the need to try to create as memorable an employee experience as possible and do their best to live each of the previous five 'Best in Class' leadership behaviours. They are not perfect; they make mistakes as after all they are human. There are, in my experience, a growing number of leaders who believe in this approach and, in their own way, are winning. They will rarely if ever make the news because they are more driven by the common good than just self-interest and are less likely to be found out because there is little to find. They know that if they get this right most of the time, this can and does lead to employees loving what they do and as a consequence a huge amount of energy and loyalty to the company. And yes they know that their employees may even 'love' them for allowing this to happen, which for many is a reward in itself.

Whether drawn from the world of sport or business, the leaders we tend to admire live these six 'Best in Class' behaviours. Here is a recap.

Table 11.1 The six 'Best in Class' behaviours: a recap

Giving not taking	Modern day leaders have understood that to create engagement the company needs to 'give out' before it takes. They believe in 'We' not 'I'.
Be self-aware	Today's great leaders are confident in what they are good at and what they are not good at. They build a team to balance their skills.
Goal orientated, not task orientated	How do we make a memorable customer experience at Christmas vs how many tills are open (of course both are needed but it's where the leader starts that matters)
Communicate to engage. Tell stories	Great bosses are great story tellers. They engage, not tell.
Be curious	Never stop learning, asking questions and being open to new ideas and perspectives.
Heart, then Head	Working hard to get strong employee and customer engagement because they know that it not only matters but it works. They lead companies that have a sustainable point of difference and are commercially successful.

Notes

1. '"Bully" Sir Philip Green under attack after sex and racism claims', *The Times*, 9 February 2019, https://www.thetimes.co.uk/article/philip-green-threatens-ex-staff-against-revealing-alleged-sexual-harassment-l7v26lpsl
2. 'Persimmon boss refuses to answer questions about £75m bonus', BBC News, 19 October 2018, https://www.bbc.co.uk/news/av/business-45911792/persimmon-boss-refuses-to-answer-questions-about-75m-bonus
3. '"Recklessness, hubris and greed" – Carillion slammed by MPs', *The Guardian*, 16 May 2018, https://www.theguardian.com/business/2018/may/16/recklessness-hubris-and-greed-carillion-slammed-by-mps
4. 'Thomas Cook boss "sorry" over collapse but defends pay and bonus', BBC News, 29 September 2019, https://www.bbc.co.uk/news/business-49869183
5. 'After Travis Kalanick's Resignation, Will Uber Really Change?' *The New Yorker*, 23 June 2017, https://www.newyorker.com/tech/annals-of-technology/after-travis-kalanicks-resignation-will-uber-really-change
6. 'Men Only: Inside the charity fundraiser where hostesses are put on show', *The Financial Times*, 23 January 2018, https://www.ft.com/content/075d679e-0033-11e8-9650-9c0ad2d7c5b5

7. Ingvar Kamprad Obituary, *The Times*, 29 January 2018, https://www.the-times.co.uk/article/obituary-ingvar-kamprad-s6rpvjfxm

8. 'Steve Jobs quotes', BrainyQuote, https://www.brainyquote.com/quotes/steve_jobs_700760

9. 'Less Is More', Wikipedia, https://en.wikipedia.org/wiki/Less_is_more

10. 'RBS reports record corporate loss', BBC News, 26 February 2009, http://news.bbc.co.uk/1/hi/business/7911722.stm

11. 'RBS Market Capitalisation', 5 November 2019, LON: RBS

12. 'Apple Market Capitalisation', 5 November 2019, apple market cap

12

Sharing the Love

Once upon a time the phrase 'Sheep Dipping' was in common parlance within business. This took a variety of forms and usually involved the employees attending a 'workshop' whereby they would be trained on or even indoctrinated into their company's new strategy. It was almost always led by the HR department and often outsourced to a training company. The idea being that the employees would leave energised, excited and engaged with the new direction. Except normally they did not. Instead, more often than not, people would leave pleased that they had had a day out of the office, but frustrated with the experience. The venue would often be a conference centre which, although functional, was rarely inspirational. The day or days would involve a lot of 'telling' with the occasional 'break-out' group whereby the employees would be asked to contribute their thoughts and views. 'Sheep Dipping' was very much the domain of leaders who occupied the middle ground of the leadership 'Love' Grid. The process would be 'head' driven with lots of rationale and with just a modicum of 'heart' to create some sense of emotional buy-in. This would take the shape of some 'ra-ra' speech from the boss, normally via a PowerPoint presentation and if the employees were really lucky a beer and a pizza at the end of the day. The HR department would then tick the box marked 'training' and employees would return to work the next day and carry on exactly as before.

In my experience every aspect of this approach is wrong, starting with the word 'workshop'. I hate this term with a vengeance as, for most people, it conjures up negative thoughts and images based on their prior knowledge. It makes sense when applied to the original meaning of a building where goods are manufactured or repaired but not when the company is trying to excite

© The Author(s) 2020
M. Cox, *The Business Case for Love*, https://doi.org/10.1007/978-3-030-36426-7_12

their employees about their future direction. So when working with my clients I deliberately use the word 'Event' to describe the experience. The Company Spirit Event or the Company Spirit Engagement Event. In my head, I liken it to going to a 'gig' whereby the experience is made up of lots of different layers all aimed at making it as memorable as possible for all those attending. A fundamental part of this is the location and type of venue, and I have to thank Duncan Bruce for this obsession. He had the firm conviction that the more unusual the space and the more it was different to a 'day at the office', the more creative and energised people would be; and he was right. A lot of time and energy would be spent in finding the right place, and this is a belief I carry to the present day. Back in the Kraft days this would usually mean finding a converted barn or a village hall. The Dairylea Event was held in Burford, in the Cotswolds, and when we went international with Estrella, we used a place not far from Lillehammer in Norway. It was winter time and the days were short and deep snow lay all around. It was a magical if slightly bizarre experience. In Germany for Bosch we used a hotel somewhere between Frankfurt and Stuttgart with a mediaeval hall-cum-dining room, and when we worked in the USA with the American Bosch team we hired a club house at a golf course north of Chicago. A couple of times we ran Events for other Nordic Kraft Teams in the archipelago, which meant a boat trip out from Vaxholm, near Stockholm, to an island where we would stay and work in a hostel. When we worked with the Norwegian Freia and Swedish Marabou teams we found a place, called Loka Brunn, almost exactly halfway from Oslo to Stockholm to make the venue as neutral as possible, given that our goal was to look for harmony and commonality in their future brand communication with no Norwegian or Swedish bias. All very different venues but all in their own way contributed to the specialness of the Event, creating long-lasting memories. Even now as I write this I can visualise each and every one of these Events, and no one involved could forget the one and only time an Event was brought abruptly to a halt when a television was put out in the hotel reception outside the room we were working in. When the first person came back from having a comfort break, the news was shared and we stopped what we were doing. All 20 or so of us stood around and stared as 9/11 unfolded in front of our eyes, seen from the perspective of Swedish television. The situation made even more improbable as we watched it standing next to a group of Russian Ramblers staying over to explore the Islands. There was no common language between us except the shared experience of watching the Twin Towers collapse.

It was not always easy to convince the client to go somewhere different and not the usual conference centre. We ran into real problems when working on a project with Mars, which insisted that their travel department sourced and booked the venue; this turned out to be a dingy hotel based not far from Schiphol Airport in Holland. The place had been chosen for convenience, with proximity to the airport the main driver. When we arrived the venue turned out to be a dark and smelly room used for who knows what strange activities. With hours to go before everyone arrived and with a panicking client on the phone we had to source something which was both inspirational and available. Thankfully, the hotel owner really helped and pointed us in the direction of a huge glasshouse set in the nearby tulip fields and disaster was averted.

In the last few years if my work is based in London, my venue of choice is Pineapple Studios, the world-famous dance studios which is still headed up by Debbie Moore. The reasons I use this are numerous. One is location as it is in the heart of Covent Garden and thus an ideal base for one of my Customer Experience Tours based around London's West End. Perhaps more important is the 'spirit' at Pineapple, as it is not just a dance studio but often the place for dance auditions for West End shows and cruise ships. This means Pineapple, named because the building used to be a pineapple warehouse around the corner from Covent Garden's original role as a fruit and vegetable market, is a place of hope and energy where the aspirants really are dancing for their 'fifteen minutes of fame'. Literally where blood, sweat and tears are shed. Last, but by no means least, is that Pineapple has strong, authentic roots with a real story attached to it. Including the little known fact that founder Debbie Moore was the very first woman to list her company on the London Stock Exchange[1] as the Chairwoman of her own company when it was floated in 1982. Something many women who are attending my Event find hard to believe given that this monumental breakthrough was so relatively recent. The last reason I use it is that it is practical, good value and with lots of space and light. I've had hundreds of people spend time with me at Pineapple and, once they relax knowing that I am not going to make them dance, the vast majority love being there.

My other obsession along with the venue is the layout of the room and, in particular, wherever possible, no central tables. People sit in a 'U' and in as relaxed a way as possible. The reason I do this is simple. People behave differently when sitting behind a table. They become more formal, more 'head' led and less creative and 'heart' led. I had known this for a long time but had it reinforced a few years back when working with the leadership team of Fat Face. For the first 80% of the Event we were based in a large open room and everything had gone swimmingly but I knew that because the hotel team needed to set up for a reception that evening, for the last couple of hours we would need to move into a small meeting room dominated by a large 'boardroom'-style table. Something remarkable happened when we had to move, which was that everyone sat down in the position that they would take in a board meeting and almost immediately became businesslike and, if truth be told, a bit boring when moments earlier in the other space the same people had been engaged and creative.

An inspiring venue with as much space and natural light as possible with a setup involving no tables are two of the ingredients needed to make a Company Spirit Event memorable. Outside space is also good as depending on the weather and the location, there is nothing quite like spending time in the fresh air to come together around the creation and story of the company's Company Spirit. Two examples come to mind, at the opposite ends of the weather spectrum. My very first client for The Company Spirit was Mats Liedholm when he was Marketing Director at Spendrups, one of Sweden's leading food and drinks companies and best known for its beer. Spendrups had bought a share in the family-owned coffee roasting company Bergstands which was based in Gothenburg and run by the hugely engaging brothers Claes and Thomas Myren. Mats' brief was a simple one: the recognition that although Spendrups knew a lot about beer, it was struggling to understand the world of coffee and what made Bergstrands unique and different. My role was to work with both the Bergstrands team and a group from Spendrups to help them create the Bergstrands Company Spirit. We ran this in February with snow still on the ground in a location down by the sea, which captured some of the mood and feel seen in Nordic Noir TV shows such as *The Bridge*. In particular, the Millennium series of books written by Stieg Larsson and the subsequent film *The Girl with the Dragon Tattoo* featuring the character Lisbeth Salander. These short days with bursts of sunshine and long evenings were the opposite to another of my favourite locations, Travaasa, not far from Austin, Texas, which was the venue for the original Neverfail Company Spirit Event. This took place weeks after Martin Mackay had become CEO, and given that this was a turnaround, it was critical for the leadership team to take a timeout to work together to create their Company Spirit. It was a spa resort, which is not normally my first choice, but given that it was October and not far from the desert, we spent much of the two days outside and this natural environment definitely helped unite a bunch of men from a range of countries with somewhat differing views and perspectives.

Those reading this who have been 'Sheep Dipped' will almost certainly have felt that they were part of an ordered process. Those leading it are on script and following a clear agenda. Those receiving it feel like they are back in the worst type of school class. Their duty is to listen and to write stuff down rather than to comment, challenge and contribute in an unscripted way. A

Company Spirit Event is different because it not only feels live, it is live. There is a structure with a beginning, middle and end to each day, but each part is governed by what those attending the Event say and do. Being live, just like performing live at a gig or in the theatre, means a lot of planning and rehearsing to make it work. The success of any Company Spirit Event is down to the preparation. As Benjamin Franklin, founding father of the USA, was fond of saying, 'By failing to prepare, you are preparing to fail'.[2] Today I still will visit any venue beforehand to make sure it is suitable, and when this is impossible, will always get there early because 9 times out of 10 whoever is in charge of setting up the room always leaves the tables as a 'boardroom' setup despite my request to the contrary. This gives me time to get the tables removed!

Whilst all these ingredients help the Event feel more memorable and the conversations and outputs richer, the signature dish is the creation of the Company Spirit. It is the very act of being involved in its birth which allows those at the original Event to start to fall in love or find their love again for the company they work for. I have described in Chap. 10 the way this happens but the reality is that 35 or so people is the maximum number who can be involved at the creation. As night follows day the next question is how to engage the rest of the organisation. Involving anything from another 50 or so people to thousands.

My approach is always the same, and let us remember a comment I made earlier in the book that the vast majority of employees want two things from their boss. They want them to offer clarity and to feel that they are actively involved in helping their company develop. To meet this need I put all employees through exactly the same experience as the original team, the only difference being that this time the Company Spirit exists. This can be up to 80–100 employees at a time. At subsequent Company Spirit Events the people attending need to leave feeling clear about what makes their company different and knowing that they are actively taking part in bringing their Company Spirit to life. There are two main levers I use to achieve this. First is to share the story of the creation of the Company Spirit with particular emphasis on the roots. Then to focus people's creativity on how to bring this to life. I do this by encouraging the teams to agree on two goals: goal one is the customer experience they want to have in a year's time and the plan to get there, and goal two, which runs in parallel, is the employee experience they want to have in a year's time and the plan to get there. This way of engaging people appeals to their hearts and heads as hearing the story of the Company Spirit sets in motion the emotional bond, whilst the building of the two plans to reach their respective goals appeals to the practical side. Everyone, after all, loves a plan, particularly one that will result in 'more money in the till' through long-term sustainable growth. The final building block is personal account-ability so that people feel it is their responsibility not somebody else's to help bring this to life through their own everyday behaviours.

These Company Spirit Engagement Events can often unleash powerful forces as for some employees this is often the first time they have been involved in this type of experience. My role also slightly changes as at these Events I am supported by three or more people from the original Company Spirit. These people, normally drawn from the leadership team, start to lead by example and show through their actions and behaviours how much they believe in their Company Spirit. We have a lot of laughs at these Events and a few tears, particularly if this is a turnaround, and people start to see a better future for their company and, of course, themselves and by inference their families. Because it's live, the unexpected can happen, as for some it is like a pressure cooker letting off steam as all the worry that they have felt during the com-pany's dark days gets released. Others, always a minority, react in a different way. For them getting clarity about what the company stands for can result in them saying, 'That's not for me', and they often leave in the following months. I always believe this to be a good thing as it shows that their personal values and the newfound company values are not aligned. It is almost impossible for someone to sit with their arms folded and not take part...although I have seen one or two try.

One thing that is certain is that these Events are never boring, as my client Matthew Main would testify. We've worked together twice. Once when Matt was Chief Operating Officer at West Cornwall Pasty Company and more recently when he was Managing Director of The Unlimited Company, which was a division of Simplyhealth. I first met Matt over a pasty and coffee at the now defunct Holborn Store. Matt had recently been hired by the CEO, Steve Gipson, who had only relatively recently started in the role with the brief to turn the company around. I knew Steve from BHS days when he was a Regional Manager and we had reconnected some years later. Matt was one of the few 'retailers' who I had met in an operational role who absolutely under-stood the people side of the business and the connection between a memora-ble employee experience, a memorable customer experience and more money in the till. Steve did as well, so I am sure that's why he hired Matt. We were on the Engagement Event part of their Company Spirit Journey when we encountered what could only be described as a cult movement involving some of the London outlets. I had first heard of this as part of my Discovery when I met with the chap who was running the outlet at Victoria Station. In essence this cult was based around members of the same 'family' only hiring people with blood connections to create an extended family. This had taken hold during the time of the previous CEO, who showed little appetite for leadership or looking after his employees. In the vacuum that this had created, some people filled it by looking after the interests of the 'family' not the interests of the company. Matt and I came face to face with the cult when they all walked in together some ten minutes after we should have started. It was more amusing than intimidating, although Matt in his opening 'Dead Important Speech' was very clear to point out where the door was in case anyone wanted to leave there and then. They didn't and the Event went as well as hoped ,although there was an undercurrent of that old English proverb 'Blood is thicker than water'. Over time, the Company Spirit filled the previous vacuum and gradually the power of the cult dissipated.

A couple of years later Matt and I teamed up again and, though there was no cult involved, this particular Company Spirit Journey certainly had some pretty big bumps in the road. This one didn't have the happy ending that was envisaged, although it had one of the most ambitious Company Spirit Visions I had helped to facilitate. The Unlimited Company was born out of a desire to be a game-changer for those people who are disabled. The existing customer experience was a poor one and the stores felt like a real example of the BBC hit comedy 'Open All Hours' with the main character shopkeeper Albert Arkwright packing his small corner grocery with as much merchandise as it will hold. The Simplyhealth Independent Living Stores and the company Simplyhealth had purchased, Care and Mobility, offered something similar. Lots of product everywhere with no thought to display, merchandising or category management. The stars of this show were the store staff who had huge product knowledge and empathy and the ability to read their customers' needs. Nothing was too much trouble for these employees. Two skills which most retailers in the UK would bite their arm off for. These stores were full of people who were real characters and loved what they did yet felt unloved by the company they worked for.

The goal of the Company Spirit was to unite the company around a common sense of purpose. To be inspired by the hugely ambitious vision of 'Life Changing' that Matt and his team set out to develop through a store experience which brought a unique, modern and contemporary approach to this category. All employees took part in a Company Spirit, and given its live nature, emotions ran high as for the first time in a long time people felt listened to and involved. People got angry and upset at points because they gave a damn.

For a number of reasons the retail side of The Unlimited Company did not work out, although the Spirit of The Unlimited Company does live on with occupational therapists involved to deliver empathy, expert advice and professional assessments to its customers. The 'Open All Hours' roots of the business made modern and relevant to the needs of today.

Love is a strong emotional and mental state. To create and share love first amongst employees and then out to customers, leaders must be able to embrace the same basic principles that make a marriage and a relationship work over the long term. A marriage starts with mutual attraction and lust, which later becomes a sense of attachment and bonding. To have a fulfilling marriage there needs to be a combination of mutual respect, honesty and commitment, communication of the regular kind, not the once-a-year kind, and collaboration. A sense of we are in this together. A Company Spirit Journey follows a similar path. The initial phase is about generating an attraction between the company and its employees, and just like in real life this can be quick to happen. To do this, these Events must provoke an emotion. A spark and frisson of excitement about the company they work for. It's what I mean by starting with the 'heart' and then following with the 'head'. Without this the relationship is more rational. More a friend than a lover. Still important but not quite the same. And not a 'Sheep Dip' in sight.

Sharing and maintaining this love is about creating the right environment to keep this flame alive. Just like in real life it is where the hard work begins to turn the initial attraction into a sense of belonging and the 'head' starts to play more of a role. The term I use to make sure this sense of belonging sticks is 'embed'. Not a phrase one would use in a marriage but it does sum up this part of the Company Spirit Journey given the need to root the Company Spirit and the subsequent behaviours in the everyday life of all employees, including the leadership team. There are four levers I recommend to my clients; so let's look at each one in turn.

Measure

'You can't measure love' and 'What gets measured gets done' seem to be conflicting statements and get those who sit in the strongly rational camp, normally the Financial Director, quite agitated. As part of the Company Spirit philosophy and approach I have tried to square the circle through explicitly connecting the link between the creation of The Company Spirit and the consequent mindset of memorable employee experiences leading to memorable customer experiences to more money in the till. Long-term sustainable commercial success. Although he probably did not realise this at the time, Stuart Owens helped to shape my thinking on this. Stuart was the FD at Fat Face when I worked with them. He and Louise Barnes were, and still are, the consummate double act. A real ying and yang of characters and skills who went on to work together again at Crew Clothing Company. Today, they are both Investor Directors in the very British online clothing brand Beaufort & Blake. Stuart and Louise are the latter-day business version of football's Brian Clough and Peter Taylor. Any discussion with Stuart was challenging as he was quick to seize on any weakness in my argument and logic. Ten years ago there were holes in my approach and he would make me face up to them and I set about trying to find simple ways of measuring love. Today I recommend to my clients a series of measures, both qualitative and quantitative, which gives first a base camp reading at the beginning of a Company Spirit Journey, and then can measure progress over the coming months and years. As I remarked in Chap. 9, I have been helped in this matter by the development and subsequent widespread use of the Net Promoter Score, which measures the link between customer satisfaction and commercial success. Given that my start point is the employees, I, along with others, have adapted this to focus on getting a simple read on how employees feel about the company they work for through people scoring on a scale of 1–10 how likely they are to recommend working at the company to a friend. Unlike NPS, my belief is that the best way to understand what is happening is to look at the raw scores in the form of a bar chart. This, in turn, can give a view on where people place themselves on the 'Love' Grid.

Scores of 9 and 10 show an employee relationship based on love. Essentially, they love what they do, feel incredibly loyal and would do anything they can to help the company succeed. A score of 7/8 shows the relationship based on respect. More a friendship than true love. Employees will still feel good about

Employee Experience	Leadership Behaviour	Employee Relationship
Memorable	Brand Heart and Head 'Let's create it together' Share	Love 9-10
Enjoyable	Retailer Head then Heart 'Please contribute to it' Shape	Respect 7-8
OK	Dealer Head led 'Just do it' Tell	Transaction 1-6

Fig. 12.1 The leadership 'Love' Grid as a measure

the company and work hard but they are less emotionally involved. Six and under means a transactional relationship, with employees working for the company because they have to and have no other choice or they are essentially there just for the money. They have very little loyalty, will go through the motions at work and will jump at the chance of moving because of a better offer. Completing this survey will tell the company what percentage of employees sit in each camp. Repeating this every year will show the shift, and if everything goes to plan an increasing number of employees will be sitting in the top part of the grid.

There are two other qualitative measures which are part of all Company Spirit Journeys. The insights from Discovery, and the score the Leadership Team gives itself vs the six 'Best in Class' company behaviours. Both happen at the beginning of a Company Spirit Journey and when repeated give an understanding of progress. What's working, what's not and what's getting in the way. Discovery in particular is a powerful tool as by getting people to talk for up to an hour on how they feel about everyday life at the Company, they are more likely to give an honest appraisal. It works on a number of levels and is invaluable for all parties involved. When the Leadership Team gets the feedback it gives a much richer account of what their employees are really feeling and why than any online employee survey can achieve. It's invaluable for me, as it not only helps connect with those who will be involved at any future Company Spirit Event but also sets the right tone of voice and shape the content of an Event. Last but not least for the employees involved they have been given a voice and feel listened to. Two examples from my work with Crew Clothing Company illustrate this point: one came out of my involvement with the 'product' teams and one a few weeks later with the 'stores' team. Discovery with the first group had highlighted a behaviour which was getting in the way of translating the original product vision set by Lisa Illis, the then Brand Director. Too many people, from designers to product development and merchandisers, expressed their views based on their opinions rather than actual insights. The consequence of this was a diversion away from the original vision of Lisa to something less clear. During the subsequent Event, the mantra 'Insights. Not Opinions' was born and became a simple message and behaviour everybody could get on board with, that is, base all comments, criticisms and suggestions on an insight not an opinion. This reduced the subjectivity involved and increased the objectivity even when discussing the highly emotional subject of what people want to wear. The consequence was that the original clarity was maintained through the product development cycle and what ended up in store was closer to what Lisa had envisioned in the first place.

A few weeks later, the Discovery with the stores teams highlighted that people knew what products they had in their store, but did not know why. The product story was not being communicated to them and therefore the store teams were lacking in the basics of product knowledge and had little confidence in their ability to advise their customers on what to buy and in particular how to put an outfit together. At their Event, the mantra 'Outfits. Not Items' was born as a clear goal for what needed to change, not least of which was to directly connect the product teams to the stores teams so that the team could feel confident in their product knowledge and their subsequent ability to allow a customer to trust the advice they were being given in order for them to walk out with a 'look' they felt confident in. This worked for both the employees and the customers. For the Crew team it was infinitely more enjoyable to spend time with their customers acting as an advisor, and the customer became more confident in the advice they were getting, and the outfit they were potentially going to buy. What is more, both these mantras were easily measurable. For the Product Teams this should result in fewer markdowns and for the stores team this should lead to a higher Average Transaction Value. For both groups, helping them become clearer in their roles increased their enjoyment in what they were doing. Who said you can't measure love?

The value of getting a team to score themselves against the 'Best in Class' company behaviours is slightly different. It's quick and subjective, and in many ways the most important measure is not the actual score, but that it has given a new framework to think about how they are behaving. It also changes the conversation and the goal away from how are we doing vs the competition to a much more aspirational one of how are we are doing against the world's best. Nevertheless, a score is a score which gets captured and allows the team to measure progress when the conversation is repeated in the following months. After all, what gets measured gets done!

Review

Reviews can take many forms, from the academic to the theatrical. In business they normally take place once or twice a year between an employee and their boss, and are generally linked to overall performance and the annual salary review. For some a successful review will form part of their bonus. In my experience they tend to focus on tangible issues, rather than intangible, that is, whether the person met the objectives set rather than how they are feeling about coming to work at the moment. In my advertising days, these reviews tended to be relaxed and often happened over a lunch or a drink. Conducting these reviews was never one of my strong points. The ultimate faux pas was when I took one of my team to lunch knowing that I was going to have to let him go. In my head, I thought this would be a civilised way of having the conversation. A bit like Roger Sterling would have dealt with the matter in 'Mad Men', namely over a dry martini. The trouble was I broke the news early in our lunch and the person involved went nuts, which meant we spent the next hour or so making small talk with him hating the sight of me. It was a bit more organised at BHS and certainly there was no alcohol involved but I was still not much better at doing this. These reviews would involve me, as the boss, answering questions about how I felt any given employee had performed and then this would be sent to the person in question via the internal mail. This was long before email. We then would arrange to meet and the person involved would offer their comments. One such situation still sticks in the memory as this particular individual arrived armed with her Tipp-Ex, which, for those you too young to remember, is a white liquid used for painting over mistakes in a piece of writing. She so vehemently disagreed with my written comments she demanded they be Tipp-Exed over there and then. A verbal battle then took place and perhaps for the best I cannot remember what conclusion we reached but I do recall it involved the Tipp-Ex being used in some way. A review of a different kind was the Balanced Score Card. I first came across this when I worked with Bosch, and whilst I understood what it was trying to do I thought that it only ever looked at what was happening through one perspective. It was what I would later call very 'head led'. It was all about recording whether objectives had been met, and in this context the word 'balanced' was a bit of a misnomer for me as there was no review of the human side. Progress or not was scored but little attempt was made to understand why.

One type of review in the context of a Company Spirit Journey is to help an individual overtly link their behaviours, as created though their Company Spirit, to their progress. I have, if I am honest, had mixed success with introducing this as a way of reviewing progress, but it can happen. The biggest barrier usually being that the HR team have already got a review process in place and are loath to change it. The greatest success at embedding this thinking was with Martin Mackay and his team at Neverfail. Working with HR Specialist Gill Mclearnon, we collectively crafted a way of reviewing the behaviour of employees and the leadership team, which was linked to both the Company Spirit and 'Best in Class' company and leadership behaviours. I haven't seen Gill since we met up at The Albany pub near Twickenham, and being Welsh she was dressed as a daffodil and ready to cheer on Wales in their match against England in the Rugby World Cup, which they duly won! Who says you can't have fun in HR?

I've had much greater success with 'review events'. Here we create a 'time-out' which can be once a quarter, once every six months or once a year. As I described in the previous chapter, teams work together to bring alive the customer experience and employee experience visions. Sometimes teams have been set up to bring to life each of the 'Best in Class' company behaviours. At other times we have held an annual Company Spirit Review Event when the team get away from the desks to take stock of progress to date and start to plan activities for the next year. Twice, Carl-Viggo Östlund took his SBAB Leadership Team to London, and what became known as London 1 and London 2 were hugely important milestones in their Company Spirit Journey. Each time we do this the rules from the original Company Spirit Event apply. An inspiring location, no tables and if possible no PowerPoints. Peter Griepenkerl Loof was a huge advocate of this approach, and we had just such a review three or so months on from the original Lansforsakringar Maklarservice Company Spirit Event in London, when I found myself at Haringe Slot near Stockholm. It was a chance to reflect on progress and a time for me to introduce the 'Best in Class' leadership behaviours shared in the previous chapter. Peter, as are most Swedes, is a great fan of fresh air and being outdoors so he and his leadership team of Jonas Stenmark, Martin Becker and Johnny Lindholm chatted about this amongst themselves in Swedish. Not in a room but whilst we all took a hike of a few kilometres to a nearby lake where we had tea and cake sitting by the water. Eighteen months later and with Peter off to a new role, his legacy lived on when all the employees were taken to Berlin to review progress and to think about and experience innovative behaviours. It was during this Event that Peter Sall, Peter's boss, and overall VD of Maklarservice and I really bonded for the first time. Over a visit to Checkpoint Charlie and a subsequent beer. The only downside of this was that that evening over dinner I was chatting to some of the younger members of the team who looked at me in disbelief when I told them I had gone through the original Checkpoint Charlie when it was still the gateway between West and East Berlin.

So where does all this take us? Reviews are important but they should not be boring. Whether it is big group 'Events' or a one-to-one review the key once again is to balance the 'heart' and the 'head'. The behaviour as driven by the Company Spirit as well as the practical plan of how to bring this alive. Most of all, these reviews show the employees that the company is serious and believes in its Company Spirit, thus helping to embed a sense of belonging to the company.

Rewards

Most employers link a review and reward in purely financial terms, and the better the review, usually against commercial and financial targets, the bigger the bonus. I grew up in a time when any bonus was contingent on the company doing well, rather than the individual. Success for a person was reflected in the size of the pay rise, not the bonus. If the targets had been met then all employees would benefit in some way, often through anything from a week's to a month's extra salary and usually paid in time for Christmas. Somewhere along the line, this morphed from a team effort to an individual effort. A good thing became a bad thing. The term 'Bankers Bonus' a catch-all for the greed and avarice at the heart of the financial crisis. It's a subject which still gets me very hot under the collar, particularly when senior executives were still earning vast sums of money when working for a bank which had been bailed out and was losing money. A lot of heated conversations have taken place over reform and greater accountability but to little avail other than to stoke the injustices I explored earlier as one of the reasons why the Establishment got a bloody nose in Chap. 2. The bonus stopped being a reward for collective success but enhances a culture of 'I', not 'we'. This is not a good image for most people, particularly when there remain so many examples of what seems reward for blatant failure.

Lynn Stout, from Cornell Law School, wrote and published the article 'Killing Conscience: The Unintended Behavioural Consequences of "Pay for Performance"' in 2014.[3] She proved what most people assumed, that the more chief executives get paid, the worse their companies perform over the next three years. She found that workplaces that rely on bonuses promote selfishness and opportunism with the end result more uncooperative, unethical and illegal employee behaviour. In other words, the exact opposite of the Business Case for Love philosophy and approach. The Institute of Leadership and Management interviewed more than 1000 managers across the economy and found that only 13% mentioned a bonus as one of the three main factors that motivated them.[4] Enjoyment of the role came top (59%), while getting along with colleagues came next (42%). A joint study in the UK and Australia by academics at the Universities of Leicester, Sydney and West Sydney[5] showed that it made better business sense to reward team performance rather than to single people out for individual bonuses. So a bit like, back in the day, when a Christmas bonus would be rewarded to all employees and only when the performance of the company justified it.

People, of course, need to earn money. We all do. Well almost all of us do. It's just that the vast, vast majority of people I have come across over the last 10 years or so of The Company Spirit have placed an equal or greater weight on their emotional reward as well as financial reward. As these academic studies confirm and to use my language, the more people love what they do and feel that they are collaborating with others, the more they will succeed. So reward in the context of The Company Spirit Journey needs to be emotional, not financial. An emotional reward can take all shapes and sizes, and for many employees, being involved in this journey is a reward in itself. I know this because people tell me. Every Company Spirit Event ends in the same way by going around the room and asking everyone to articulate what they 'learned and enjoyed' from the preceding experience. It's a way of creating closure for the Event as everyone contributes their own individual thoughts. It's also a good way for whoever the 'boss' is to hear from their team how they are feeling. I've probably listened to well over a couple of thousand people share their views in this way, and the vast majority of the 'enjoys' relate in some way to the venue, the experience, but more than any other the sense of listening and working with their fellow employees. Their reward was to be part of it.

This is why having the mindset of creating a memorable employee experience is fundamental to the success of a company if it is serious in embedding the Company Spirit and sharing the love throughout. Clarity, empathy, engagement and involvement are the main building blocks for this, which can be enhanced considerably by the environment people work in. Food can play a big part in this, which is something that the upstart Silicon Valley companies have always been known for. Google in particular put a great emphasis on food with employee No. 53, the chef Charlie Ayers[6] who was charged with creating an offer of wholesome food which would be free for everyone working at Google. Long before Google was even a glint in the eye, Scandinavian companies have understood the value of food as part of the employee experience. In the early days a visit to Estrella in Gothenburg, Kraft in Stockholm or the Kraft office in Oslo, which was next to the Freia chocolate factory, always meant a trip to the canteen where I quickly learnt one of the idiosyncrasies which separated the Norwegians from the Swedes. For the former lunch was normally served cold such as an open sandwich and for the latter invariably it was hot, such as a fish stew. More recently I have had many a hearty meal at the canteen at Lansforsakringar.

Alongside food, Nordic companies seem to place a greater emphasis on the design of the working environment, and this is particularly true of the office of my client Lansforsakringar Maklarservice. Since the time of my first involvement, Peter Sall and Anders Lofthammar, who succeeded Peter

Griepenkerl Loof, have transformed the office for their team. It's a really smart and cleverly designed working environment which encompasses team areas, meeting areas, work stations and quiet places depending on the needs of the day, and whilst I claim no direct credit it certainly helps to bring alive and embed their Company Spirit. In the UK, the McLaren Technology Centre stands head and shoulders above any UK client in their understanding of how the environment people work in and the food they serve helps create a memorable employee experience which is in turn part of the emotional reward people get from working there.

Another way to reward employees as part of their Company Spirit Journey is to inspire people. This too can take many forms from the everyday to the set piece. Bringing together all of the Crew Store managers for the launch of what was called 'Crew Connect' at Twickenham, the home of English rugby, was for all those involved pretty awe-inspiring. People did not have to be rugby fans to be wowed by sitting alongside the pitch and looking upwards to the stands towering above. Living the motto 'Be Out. Not In' and encouraging employees to get out from behind their desks helps people gain fresh insights and perspectives, and is a reward in itself, as is receiving regular updates on what is happening but in a relaxed and enjoyable manner. Martin Mackay is a pass master at this, and at all three companies I have known him at, he has created some form of 'Martin's Musings'. Written in a style which is a sort of mashup from *Private Eye*, the satirical magazine; *Wisden Cricketers' Almanack* and *Business Week*, it was a weekly roundup of what is happening within the company and kept people engaged and hopefully, in a small way, inspired by the company they were working for.

I am not sure we will see the end of the 'Bonus Culture' anytime soon, particularly within the banking sector, which has largely lived out the maxim of the three wise monkeys, 'see no evil, hear no evil, speak no evil', since 2008. I do see change elsewhere which is more often than not driven by the employees who see going to work as much more than just money, and who place as much if not more emphasis on the emotional reward as the financial reward. Best in class leaders understand this motivation and look at rewarding their employees in ways that reflect this need.

Teeth

Back in Chap. 8, I introduced the idea of 'Personal Values and Company Values Match' as one of my six 'Best in Class' company behaviours. For me it is a truism that the clearer and stronger the culture the easier it is for individual employees to know whether they fit, and if they fit they tend to stay because they love what they do and the company they work for. As Fortune's Human Capital 30 list published in 2016[7] highlights, the companies with the clearest cultures are rewarded with extremely low employee turnover rates. This makes sense given that these companies already have a strong culture and have no doubt recruited in their own way for a mixture of 'fit' as well as 'skills'. Given that most of my work is either with turnarounds or in some way putting more 'heart into the company', how do employees react as their company embeds their Company Spirit and along the way strengthens its culture.

In the broadest of terms three clear groups emerge. The first and biggest, usually around 50% of employees, react with a combination of relief and excitement and do their best to embrace their newfound Company Spirit through changing their own behaviours. There is normally another 25% who sit on their hands. Neither for nor against but waiting to see, perhaps because they have been 'Sheep Dipped' in the past and are a bit cynical about the need to change. The final 25% or so can struggle. Either because they do not believe in the Company Spirit or because they resist the need to change. They remain as the 'frozen middle layer'. This percentage split can often apply to the leadership team as well, and I have yet to be involved in a Company Spirit Journey where there hasn't been at least one change relatively quickly after the original Event. The make-up of the SBAB Leadership attending London 2 was different to London 1 as Carl-Viggo Ostlund shuffled his pack with people joining who would share his vision. Over the course of the first year of the journey, the churn rate can be quite high as employees start to make sense of the new environment. For those loving it, the relationship gets stronger. Those at the other end of the spectrum start to leave; some of their own accord, others because they are asked to. For those who choose to leave this is often because they are now clear on what their company stands for and have come to the view that their personal values and the company's values do not align. This does not mean they are poor at their job or a bad person but is more a recognition that they would be happier in another culture. Those in the 'sitting on hands' group tend to start to make up their minds, one way or the other. This is where the other three levers make their mark. Through using the measures, reviews and rewards as suggested, these people start to see that the company and those around them are changing. They might struggle to make the changes required but they see the direction of travel and start to ask for help so that they can align. It is the last group who are the real problem. Those who don't like what is happening but don't go perhaps because they are scared of the unknown or because they feel that they are sufficiently good at their job to feel that they will not be challenged. This group can become quite vocal and disruptive and undermine the confidence of others, which is why I call the fourth lever 'teeth'.

This is not about mass sackings but it is about making it quite clear that behaviours which are not in line with the Company Spirit will not be tolerated, and a refusal by the employee to change can result in being asked to leave the company. Being in love as we all know only works if the feeling is mutual. 'Unrequited love' as George Sands notes, 'differs from mutual love, just like delusion differs from the truth'.[8] So it is with a company. If it is doing its best to be loved, then those who reject the overtures cause only pain and division. Difficult as this may be, again, just as in a marriage the two necessary steps are 'counselling' whereby time is to devoted to getting to the root cause of the issue and if that doesn't work 'divorce' is probably the best outcome, which, of course, reinforces in the minds of those employees who love what they do that the Company Spirit really does matter.

Sharing the love takes time, dedication and devotion. Each of my clients has adapted the four levers of measure, review, reward and teeth to suit their own circumstances. The ultimate reward is to create a company that is thriving not just surviving. Viewing business as a social system operated by people for people. To care. A company that knows sustainable success or failure depends on the quality of relationships both inside and outside the company. A company that wants to be bragged about.

A company that wants you to love them.

Notes

1. 'Debbie Moore', Wikipedia, https://en.wikipedia.org/wiki/Debbie_Moore
2. 'Benjamin Franklin quotes', BrainyQuote, https://www.brainyquote.com/quotes/benjamin_franklin_138217
3. Stout, Lynn A. 'Killing Conscience: The Unintended Behavioral Consequences of "Pay for Performance"', Cornell University of Law School Spring 2014, https://pdfs.semanticscholar.org/ca98/e92387b81d63f3fa995be7f2d-f01a4ac383a.pdf
4. 'Beyond the bonus: driving employee performance', the Institute of Leadership and Management, https://www.institutelm.com/resourceLibrary/beyond-the-bonus-driving-employee-performance.html
5. 'Study finds final year individual bonuses are counter-productive', University of Leicester, 24 November 2015, https://www2.le.ac.uk/offices/press/press-releases/2015/november/study-finds-final-year-individual-bonuses-are-counter-productive

6. Charlie Ayers, Wikipedia, https://en.wikipedia.org/wiki/Charlie_Ayers
7. 'Human Capital 30: Companies that Put Employees Front and Venter', Fortune, 8 March 2016 https://fortune.com/2016/03/08/human-capital-30/
8. 'George Sands quotes', Wise Old Sayings, http://www.wiseoldsayings.com/unrequited-love-quotes/

13

Creating Your Own Love Story

This is the summary chapter. It outlines the steps and the order they need to be taken in, to create love amongst employees and customers and for the company to be bragged about.

The journey starts with one simple question and goes to the heart of the ambitions of the CEO and his or her leadership team. Where do we want to be on the 'Love' Grid? If the answer is at the top then that is wonderful news. But there must be a real desire and energy to want to do this. Do not fake it. It is better not to start on the journey than to pretend. Being at the top of the 'Love' Grid is tough but very rewarding. Not every CEO has the leadership, behavioural skills or belief to do this. They must be able to live or aspire to live all of the six 'Best in Class' leadership behaviours, and whilst this is the same for the rest of the leadership team, primary responsibility must be with the CEO. As we have seen throughout the book and when we look at everyday business life, so many businesses fail because of the attitude of the boss. Do not make the mistake of creating a set of values which sit on the website but are not acted upon. That is not 'The Business Case for Love'. The worst mistake a CEO can make is to aspire to be at the top of the 'Love' Grid whilst behaving at the bottom as a 'Dealer'. It will end in tears. First the employees will see through this and then the customers will.

So assuming the ambition, drive, energy and belief are all in place, what are the steps on the journey? From a timing perspective there are three main phases of a Company Spirit Journey.

Phase 1, the 'kick-off' phase, is quick and is usually achieved within six weeks. The sooner the better as experience suggests that the quicker people embrace a common sense of purpose and language, the faster the benefits are

© The Author(s) 2020
M. Cox, *The Business Case for Love*, https://doi.org/10.1007/978-3-030-36426-7_13

felt…leading to a more memorable employee experience, a more memorable customer experience and more money in the till.

Phase 2, engaging the whole of the company with the Company Spirit, usually takes a couple of months.

Phase 3, embedding the Company Spirit and bringing it to life, is over the course of a year.

Please remember that cultural change is a marathon not a sprint!

For the full value of the approach to be realised, there needs to be a commitment by senior management to embedding, rewarding and measuring behaviours in line with their Company Spirit.

Let's looking at each phase in turn.

Phase 1: 'The Kick-Off'

Step 1: Discovery: What's the Gap and Why?

Discovery is a series of one-on-one conversations lasting up to an hour each. The goal is to talk to as many people as possible in order to gain a real sense of current everyday life. What is working? What is not? What is getting in the way? This can only be achieved by talking and listening to a wide range of people covering different levels, different functions and different periods of time at the company. In the case of companies operating in different countries, visits to each would need to be arranged. Skype and FaceTime have a role but it is never the same as being truly face to face.

There are two main benefits to Discovery:

- The 'jigsaw puzzle' is created. This helps form the 'cold shower of reality' which reflects current everyday life and the gaps between any stated values and the actual employee and customer experience. It summarises where the business is today and how the business currently behaves in the context of the six 'Best in Class' company behaviours. It creates a measure.
- The second benefit is to engage the employees with the journey ahead. If people feel listened to and their views are understood they are much more likely to believe in the Company Spirit Journey and their role in bringing it to life

Discovery insights also give shape and tone to the Company Spirit Event.

Step 2: The Company Spirit Event

A two-day Event with a highly collaborative feel. Aimed at giving people fresh perspectives and insights and ultimately to inspire people about the company they work for and their part in creating a sustainable future.

When working with a European company this is normally in London at One Alfred Place (www.onealfredplace.com) and Pineapple Studios in Covent Garden (http://www.pineapple.uk.com/studio_hire/default.aspx).

To include all members of the Senior Management Team plus key influences (up to 20 people).

Why London?

As a Londoner, I may be a bit biased but it is one of the most creative and inspirational cities in the world to have as a backdrop to my work. The goal is to get the team away from their day job and to a place full of energy. To gain fresh insights, fresh perspectives and experiences which will inspire them to think and behave differently. In other words, to create a memorable experience which the team will 'love'.

There are no formal breaks. Coffee and lunch and the evening is on 'the go' and is part of the experience.

In advance of the Event, all those attending will have a little light homework.

Each person is expected to think about and be prepared to talk about bringing a company, brand or customer experience they 'love' to life visually (i.e. a page from the website etc.).

The Event starts with capturing the 'heart'. It will be a tailormade 'experience' where the team take off their company 'hat' and put on their own customer hat.

The Event kicks off at 9am with a short but powerful 'Dead Important Speech' by the CEO which outlines the importance of the Event in opening minds, sharing experiences and then creating a plan, based on a set of employee- and customer-focussed behaviours which are owned by everybody.

There is then a collective discussion on companies and brands people 'love' and why, 'What makes a memorable customer experience?' and what are the 'Best in Class' behaviours companies adopt to get both their employees and customers to love their brand based on people's own experience.

This will act as context and backdrop and as an introduction both to the six 'Best in Class' company behaviours and to a 'tool' that links internal behaviour with the external customer experience and relationship (the 'Love' Grid).

Then with the team split into small groups of four the main focus of the day (four hours) will be getting people out into central London and to feel and experience how other 'Best in Class' companies deliver a memorable experience. This 'session' will encompass a range of tasks and experiences all aimed at seeing how other organisations take a different approach in how they use their brand values and behaviours to engage with their customers and create their own version of 'memorable customer experiences'.

The actual experiences will be agreed post 'Discovery' but experience suggests that they will originate from 'Best in Class' brands such as Apple, Aesop, Nespresso, Whole Foods Store, Niketown and Hamleys.

Returning to the location, the team comes back together and shares their experiences (both good and bad). As a group we will then agree what insights are helpful for the team. It is recommended that drinks and dinner be held at One Alfred Place.

The Next Day should be a milestone day in the life of the company. The day starts with a brief recap of company goals and objectives to remind the team of the opportunity for the company. This acts as a backdrop to the centrepiece of the Event…creating the Company Spirit.

Using the 'Company Spirit' model as a guide, we will together create a common language and set of beliefs based on bringing alive the company story (its roots) and use that as an anchor for creating an inspiring and clear vision for the customer experience.

Passion brings alive the employee experience.

Telling the story of a company (ups and downs, from a human perspective) is an incredibly powerful way of turning up the volume on how people feel. It adds 'heart' to the Company!

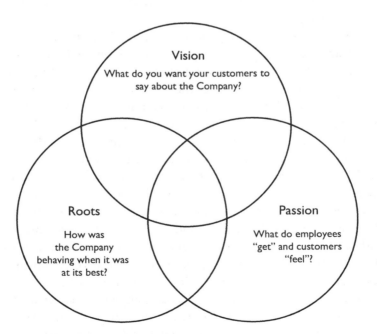

Fig. 13.1 The Company Spirit model

Finally, using the newly created Company Spirit and all the experiences and insights gained during the London Customer Experience plus a reminder of current everyday life through Discovery the team will work on two 'visions'.

1. What is the Employee Experience we want to have in a year's time and what are the first steps we need to take to get there?
2. What is the Customer Experience we want to have in a year's time and what are the first steps we need to get there?

The outputs from the Company Spirit Event should be:

1. The team having thought differently and experienced 'Best in Class' company behaviours and then seen their company within that context
2. A common sense of purpose, language and clarity on what the brand stands for that connects the company's values, behaviours and goals, via the Company Spirit, to the employee and customer experiences and fosters an entrepreneurial and innovative culture
3. The importance of 'Roots' (the Company story) as a way of engaging people, both old and new, and anchoring the company 'difference'
4. A plan to close the gap between how the Senior Management Team wants to behave and how it is currently behaving.
   And hopefully, a team excited and inspired for the engagement journey ahead.

Step 3: 'Making Sense of It' Review

The core team review the outputs and agree on next steps. By this stage, we should have

1. A team that is excited, inspired and with an intuitive sense and a much broader understanding of the company difference and how to create memorable employee and customer experiences
2. An understanding of what support and coaching the Senior Management Team need to first live the Company Spirit themselves and then engage and then embed the plan amongst all employees
3. Knowledge of what measures, reviews and rewards need to be put in place to celebrate success
4. The appointment of sponsors and the establishment of the principle of cross-functional teams appointed to bring to life both the Employee and Customer Experience Visions.

Now on to phase 2!

Phase 2: Engaging the Company with the Company Spirit

- Bringing alive the Company Spirit
- Bringing alive the Customer Experience and Employee Experience Visions
- The Company Spirit Engagement Kit
- 'Train the Trainers'
- Company Wide Company Spirit Engagement Events that create a sense of belief in the company they work for, personal accountability and clarity on how to bring alive this mindset though their roles.

Phase 3: Embedding the Company Spirit

In addition to 'formal' quarterly reviews to monitor progress of the two Company Spirit Teams (the customer experience team and the employee experience team), the core team need to agree and introduce these four 'levers':

- Measure: What measures do we want to review progress, for example, employee engagement and customer engagement scores (in addition to Discovery and scores vs 'six Best in Class' company behaviours)?
- Review: to add Company Spirit behaviours to individual employee reviews to drive personal accountability
- Reward: to reward and celebrate behaviours (big or small) in line with the Company Spirit
- Teeth: exiting those who do not want to live the Company Spirit.

Overall Outputs

- The Company's Company Spirit and its difference brought alive through everyday behaviours amongst the Senior Management Team and ultimately all employees in a way that all employees get and customers feel
- Clarity around what the company stands for so that 'image' and 'experience' match
- The gaps highlighted through Discovery closed
- A Company with an approach which starts with 'What is the customer experience we are trying to create?' and works backwards to develop products and services which meet those needs

- A constant stream of innovation and entrepreneurial thinking with which to stimulate growth
- A company which judges itself against 'Best in Class' (e.g. Apple and Google) rather than the category
- A company which remembers to look after and value its customers and its people as it grows
- Employees who love what they do, which leads to customers who love the company and are happy to brag about it to others, leading to more 'money in the till' in a sustainable way
- The leadership team equipped and confident to be seen as living and leading the behaviours and balancing the 'heart' and the 'head'.

And last, but by no means least, people recruited with a balance of cultural fit as well as skills and capabilities.

Appendix: Some Love Stories

Louise Barnes, Investor Director at Beaufort & Blake (Previously CEO of Fat Face and Crew Clothing Company)

'I have worked with Marc Cox and Company Spirit in three different businesses, and on both projects he has made a huge difference to our brand clarity and ultimately commercial success. This is not fluffy HR stuff, it's about helping you as a business to identify your authenticity, link it with your values, give your customers and employees something to believe in and then everything you do can be linked back to your roots.

He doesn't give you opinions, he conducts research among your employees and customers and plays it back to you. It doesn't pull any punches, but it's what you knew deep down.

If you decide to act on it, there's then a collaborative and inclusive approach to making a change. It's authentic because the answer will come from within your business, Marc will just help you tease it out. The process is simple, fun and transformative. And having seen its results, my FD is now one of Marc's biggest fans!

I can guarantee I will be back again, it's magic'.

© The Author(s) 2020
M. Cox, *The Business Case for Love*, https://doi.org/10.1007/978-3-030-36426-7

Carl-Viggo Östlund (Co-owner of Juvinum, Board Member of a Number of Scandinavian Companies and Previously CEO of SBAB)

'Some years ago I was given the task to lead a conversion of a leading mortgage bank into a full assortment bank. The strategy behind this conversion was to retain existing customers, but being able to recruit new customers who were looking for more than only mortgage.

Early on in the strategic process the management team and I understood that the world does not need another full assortment bank, but the world needs a bank that is acting differently in their relationship with customers. Banks are facing one common problem wherever you go in the world and that is low or very low customer confidence. The financial crisis that are occurring on a regular basis have not really helped in improving the customer confidence, the banks actions have been very erratic and customer unfriendly.

When the management team and I started the strategic work we early on realized that our focus should be on customer experience in order to make a difference. Now in hindsight I am convinced that I would come to the same conclusion all over again. In this process I was introduced to Marc Cox by an old friend of mine. We met for breakfast at a downtown hotel in Stockholm and Marc introduced me to the "Business Case for Love". I have to confess that initially I was a bit amused or confused, you don't talk about love in business! However, when I understood the full meaning of the concept, I really took it to heart and engaged Marc in our strategic work.

The difficult parts in creating sustainable customer experience are focus and to maintain an outside-in thinking of what the company is doing or selling. Marc Cox was instrumental in keeping us focused in our strategic work to create a memorable experience for our customers in an industry with very poor customer experience. Marc accompanied us in the process and lead two London Company Spirit Events for the management team. Today, the learning from that process is very much alive with me in my functions on various boards of directors and operational work in companies in very different industries'.

Martin Mackay (Worked with Marc on Three Occasions as a Client of 'The Business Case for Love' and in Particular as the Former CEO of the Neverfail Group and the Experior Group)

'Marc and I met several years ago when I attended a "Business Case for Love" taster event; from there we have developed a personal and professional relationship that is one of the most inspiring and fruitful of my career.

The concept of "The Company Spirit" is one of the most powerful I have ever worked with and it has been at the heart of the transformation of two companies I have run. To improve business performance, every company needs to understand what is at the heart of its success in terms of vision, passion and behaviour. Vision is defined in terms of what the company wants customers to say when asked about their relationship; passion in terms of the core focus, belief and reason for existing (the proverbial "why"); behaviour in terms of how the company operates when at its best.

Marc's process to define the Company Spirit makes it completely authentic because it comes from the employees (management and staff alike) as they tell the company story. This creates an emotional engagement with the Company Spirit which makes it the guiding beacon for defining strategy, execution and critical business decisions. Marc's experience, empathy, creativity, vision and insight facilitate and inform the process of developing the Company Spirit but never define it – that it comes from the company itself is what makes it so powerful.

From the Company Spirit comes a very simple mantra: create a memorable employee experience and the results will follow. This is no meaningless definition of values with no business impact. On the contrary it is designed to deliver real results from business transformation. The Company Spirit defines how the company (and management in particular) should behave; then the focus is on driving employee engagement; engaged employees deliver a better service which will win business; the memorable customer experience follows.

For leaders who want to grow themselves, expand their teams' horizons and give them new perspectives, and deliver extraordinary results, engaging Marc to create "the business case for love" could not have a greater endorsement from me'.

Mats Liedholm (Currently MD of Fazer Lifestyle Foods)

'The Business Case for Love and the Company Spirit are both easily accessible tools in creating a core sense of purpose for any company with ambitions of creating a memorable customer experience. I have witnessed the impact many times, working with everything from the small Gothenburg based coffee company Bergstrands Kaffe to the large multinationals, like Kraft Foods. Engaging with Marc, he has a wonderful ability to create a strong and positive atmosphere with any group, he leads the teams through the wonderfully accessible tools making the team understand and appreciate as well as remember the key building blocks in creating something out of the ordinary. If you do have the opportunity to experience the company spirit in London, really appreciating what a truly strong company spirit is all about, but also to sadly witness the opposite, you are in a strong position to take the destiny of your company in your owns hands. Marc will guide you, he will challenge you and he will constantly remind you what good looks like and it is worth every minute spent'.

Mathew Main (Twice Client of The Company Spirit. First at West Cornwall Pasty Company Then When MD at The Unlimited Company, Part of Simplyhealth)

'I have worked with Marc on two separate occasions, once in a pure turnaround environment and once in a business that was the sum of numerous acquisitions. There was an absolute need to unify both businesses; one where the business had suffered from poor leadership and needed to rebuild and reconnect with its purpose and the other that needed to establish a strong identity to ensure the business could deliver on its strategic ambitions.

The methodology Marc applies in facilitating the people within the business to discover their company spirit has delivered on both occasions. The connection with the roots of the company and understanding the impact of behaviours on delivering a memorable experience links to create a powerful engine to drive cultural change and ultimately improved business performance.

The results achieved have been exemplary in both instances. The first business, a food to go retailer, saw huge improvements in the colleague and customer experience. Colleague turnover which historically ran at over 42% fell to just below 30% and customer compliments increased by 200% with complaints reducing by 25%. Improved consistency of team members allowed overall labour spend to reduce by 18% and sales which had been on a downward trajectory on like for like basis recovered to single digit growth in a 6 month period.

The company spirit experience delivers. The link between colleague and customer experience and business performance has been long proven; Jack Welch of GE once described the three key focuses for a business as being customer experience, employee experience and cash flow. The methodology Marc applies truly enables the team that are the company to create and identify with their company spirit. Furthermore, once the company spirit is alive, Marc works with the people in the business to enable a cycle of continual revisit to keep the company spirit fresh for everyone.

I have thoroughly enjoyed working with Marc on both occasions. Marc is a consummate professional and works tirelessly with the business to support bringing the company spirit to life throughout the organisation. Marc has the ability to effortlessly switch between engaging with front facing customer service teams through to supporting the executive in building and refining strategy. The results that have been delivered for both businesses were in no small part a result of Marc's support and focus. I would not hesitate recommending Marc to any business looking to deliver great results through reconnecting with their roots, their people, and their customers'.

Index

© The Author(s) 2020
M. Cox, *The Business Case for Love*, https://doi.org/10.1007/978-3-030-36426-7

9783030364250